I Wore the Ocean
in the Shape of a Girl

A MEMOIR

Kelle Groom

FREE PRESS

New York   London   Toronto   Sydney

FREE PRESS
A Division of Simon & Schuster, Inc.
1230 Avenue of the Americas
New York, NY 10020

First Free Press hardcover edition June 2011

FREE PRESS and colophon are trademarks of Simon & Schuster, Inc.

For information about special discounts for bulk purchases, please contact Simon & Schuster Special Sales at 1-866-506-1949 or business@simonandschuster.com.

The Simon & Schuster Speakers Bureau can bring authors to your live event. For more information or to book an event contact the Simon & Schuster Speakers Bureau at 1-866-248-3049 or visit our website at www.simonspeakers.com.

DESIGNED BY ERICH HOBBING

The author is grateful to the editors of the following publications in which excerpts first appeared, sometimes in different forms: *AGNI, Bloomsbury Review, Brevity, Ploughshares, New Madrid, Opium, West Branch,* and *Witness.*

Manufactured in the United States of America

3   5   7   9   10   8   6   4   2

Library of Congress Cataloging-in-Publication Data
Groom, Kelle.
I wore the ocean in the shape of a girl: a memoir / Kelle Groom.
p. cm.
Includes bibliographical references.
1. Groom, Kelle.   2. Poets, American—21st century—Biography.
3. Grief—Biography.   4. Alcoholism—Biography.   I. Title.
PS3607.R64Z46 2011
811'.6—dc22
[B]   2010048931
ISBN 978-1-4516-1668-2
ISBN 978-1-4516-1670-5 (ebook)

for Tom

. . . though the earth tried to hold each one of them upright,
saying don't imagine don't imagine
there has been another like you—

—Brenda Hillman,
"Small Spaces"

Charon

You who pull the oars, who meet the dead,
who leave them at the other bank, and glide
alone across the reedy marsh, please take
my boy's hand as he climbs into the dark hull.
Look. The sandals trip him, and you see,
he is afraid to step there barefoot.

—Zonas, 1st century BC,
translated by Brooks Haxton

Contents

Contents

I Wore the Ocean
in the Shape of a Girl

Evidence of Things Unseen

Morphine makes me weightless, airborne. Like a spider. I rest in a corner of the high ceiling, look down on my body on the white hospital bed. It is just one shot, one needle through my skin. But even nine months pregnant, my frame is small—the weight all baby. So the effect of the drug is a flood in my veins. I'd like to walk down the street feeling this light. I'd like to be a passenger in a dusty car on a dirt road, and see a veil of trees, the clearing inside. Graveyard of cars arranged in a kind of circle. All the engines lifted out, windows dull with dirt. In that clearing I know I could find evidence of things unseen. Me on the bed waiting for my cervix to be effaced. Waiting to open like a door, ten centimeters. Then I can push.

"I can't believe you did this twice," I say to my mother after I come down from the ceiling, and a truck stuck in the sand guns it below my belly button. Digs in, stalls, digs. My mother laughs.

"You forget," she says. Pulls her chair closer. We're both mothers now. In the circle that the bed makes for us, she's not mad at me for not marrying, not appalled by my sexuality, my basic biology, my lack of restraint. She's helping me count contractions, her knees a few inches away from me in her beige pantsuit. One of the outfits she wears to teach first grade. At school, the children all sit in a circle around her. Once, her school gave her an award; they took her picture as she leaned against a tree, smiling. Now it's 1981. Despite the pain, I'm happy to be here with her. There's an easiness, as if we're on a brief vacation together, like friends. She's younger than I am now, about to hold her first grandchild, about to let me give him away. My mom will never touch him again. She'll blow up the snapshot of my son that my aunt and uncle will mail to us, frame it, place it on the dresser in her bedroom. The enlarging process increasing the light in the photo, so that he's surrounded by glowing circles, like snow is falling on him at night.

My son has his eyes closed now. He's close to leaving my nineteen-year-old body. Ripples wash over his skin that no one has ever touched, except me. We're still together. My darkness keeps him safe, fed. My body does everything right: carrying, feeding, singing a water song. My heart counted on like a lullaby. In the outside world, my practical skills are limited—I don't know how to keep house or manage money, sometimes I can barely speak. But in my son's world, my body has everything he needs. I belong to him.

I'd had an overwhelming need to push for what felt like a long time, but the nurses kept saying it was too early, "Don't push." When a nurse looks between my legs, she's surprised. "The baby's coming," she says. "Push." Her tone is controlled but urgent. They need to move fast. The medical people still have to get me into the delivery room. They scoot me onto a rolling bed, push me down the hall into another room. My mother goes to sit with my dad in the waiting room. I don't know who decides I'm going to do this alone. Even my own doctor isn't on duty. The hands that lift me are speedy, rushed. My bare feet are put into cold metal stirrups, which feels frightening. As if something is about to happen that I will not be able to stand unless I am restrained. A lamp is flood-light bright. I'm glad to push. A couple of minutes go by. I scream once. It's a surprise—no planning, no slow intake of breath. The pain is surprising; my skin about to rip open from my baby's head pushing out. The threshold keeps being raised. I scream again when I tear. And my son is in the world. I thought he would be red with blood or white or wrinkled. Maybe they washed him before I saw him? His skin looks like the skin on apricots. It might have been all the carrot juice I drank. He looks as if he's had a life-time of good meals.

Then, they take him away. It's probably strange to him too, the first time we've parted since he was an unseen spiral twirl-ing inside. A doctor takes a needle and thread and sews me up. I've been given a numbing shot, but I can still feel the tug of each stitch. The way he makes it tight.

Nurses lift me onto a rolling bed again, take me into a ward of the Navy hospital. One side of the hall is maternity; the other side for women with gynecological problems. Our side is lit up, shining. I fall asleep. But in a few hours, a nurse wakes me up. "Your baby's hungry." My body weeps as if a horse had kicked me between my legs, or bitten me with its huge horse teeth. I am sure that no one in my state should stand up. "You need to stand up," the nurse repeats. "Your baby needs to eat. It's been four hours." My hospital gown is a bloom around my body. I sit up. My feet hang off the bed, and the nurse gives me her arm. She doesn't smile. She's a Navy nurse, a member of the military. I can feel a pool inside my body, a slosh of blood. My breasts leak through my gown. I clutch the nurse's arm. My feet cold on the floor. She walks.

I follow her down the middle of the hall to a room of glass, where we turn right, until we come to a room without glass, a door. I stand inside, teetering beside a sink. Rocking chairs behind me against the wall. "Wait here." She leaves. She comes back with my baby. He is wrapped in a white blanket, that material that feels as if it has clouds in it, hilly and airy at the same time. Someone has wrapped my baby's hands in white gauze, so he won't scratch his face with his fingernails. The nurse points to the sink, the pHisoderm. I soap myself, rinse. Pat my hands dry with a brown paper towel.

My baby's eyes are still closed, and they're big. The arc of his eyelids are little beds where I rest my eyes. He's the most peaceful baby I have ever seen. It's Mom, I want him to know without my saying so. The nurse doesn't know he's being adopted. She doesn't know the mistake she's making. The doctor will come to me later and say I can't hold my baby again, can't feed him. "It could cause you permanent emotional damage," he says. I'm in the TV room when he walks in to tell me this. It's night. The doctor's day is done, but he wants to let me know this now, so I won't expect to feed my son again. *The Greatest American Hero* is on the TV screen. The actor has the curly yellow hair of an angel, flying around to help people out. "Can I still look at him through the glass?" I ask. The doctor acquiesces. "But just once a day," he says. I'm in the hospital for three days. And it's only this day, this morning, that the nurse will say, "Hold your arms like this," as she holds my son close to her chest. And then she holds him out to me.

Her arms are like bridges, transporting my son to me in this breathing world. I feel as though my vision could fill with white clouds at any moment, that I could fall to the floor. I feel that someone should be steadying me. But then the weight of him is in my hands. And it is like carrying him inside my body—something I already know how to do. There is no thought of letting go. The bones in my arms use all their hardness, my blood, my skin itself, all the force in my body holds him, will keep him safe against any harm. My legs are metal. "You can sit in the rocking chair," the nurse says. I relax against the cushion beneath me, the chair's wooden bars supporting my back like little trees. "Hold his head up," she says, and hands me a bottle. The nurse leaves. We're quiet. My son and I like it, not rushing. I introduce myself for real: "It's Mom." He likes me. I place the bottle on his little rose mouth, let him take the nipple in his mouth. But he's not hungry yet. A little milk comes out on his lips. I don't know how much time I have. I say, his name, "Tommy." I'm the first one to call him by his name. I say, "I love you." I want to take my time, tell him everything. But he's so content. We rock a little. Hang out. We would have been so good together with silences. The nurse comes back.

I never feed him again. No matter how many Kleenexes I put in my bra cups, despite the pills I take to dry up my milk, it leaks through all my clothes. My small breasts become so heavy and hard they are like mini basketballs. I could feed ten babies with this milk. During the day, a nurse brings a heat machine, a bright electric sun, and shines it between my legs to dry my stitches. The curtains are drawn. I can hear my aunt and uncle outside the cloth, the joking about my suntanning machine. They are kind, jubilant to become my baby's parents. His eyes are still closed. During the day, I break the doctor's rule and stand at the glass for every feeding. I dismiss the doctor's warning about causing damage to myself. I need to see my son. It's like the need to push when he was being born. There's no choice. Watch a nurse hold my boy in her arms. Sometimes she stands while she feeds him, sometimes she sits. When she's standing, she holds him up high, as if showing him to someone—a king. Here he is. The nurses scowl at me. But what can they do? One nurse comes to me at night, opens my curtain. She sits on my bed as if she is my friend. "Would you like to talk?" she asks. "No," I say. Maybe she was doing something extra, trying to be nice, helpful. But I am in no mood for pity. At the glass, I watch the nurse give my son a bottle, my breasts leaking dark quarters through my bra, my gown. I stand there, and watch him held in her hard arms and think, I can do that. I can do that.

On the fourth day, I am discharged. The air is tense when my family arrives—my mother and father, my aunt and uncle— because they are afraid. They are afraid that I will take him in my arms and not let go. That we will hitch a ride out of town, and I will bleed all over the front seat, massaging my uterus with one hand. Trying to bring it back to size. Calm the blood down. My breasts have all the food my son needs. And finally he'll be able to latch on, to relieve this pressure, this store of milk I've been saving for him. The nurse shows my aunt and uncle my son's belly button, she explains how to care for it, where we connected. She opens his blanket to do this, my naked boy. My aunt has clothes for him. She has a baby snowsuit. It envelops him in cushy plastic. Like an Eskimo baby. My mom is motioning me out of the way. But the nurse who never smiled, she says, "No matter who is adopting the baby, the mother takes him out of the hospital." The mother, the mother. That's me. I'm visible again. It's a rule, so no one can disagree. I make my arms into the shape of a cradle. The nurse places my son in my arms. His snowsuit is soft and puffy. He looks comfortable nestled in there, eyes closed. I'm not yet afraid of doing anything wrong, of holding on to him. I know this is just for a few moments, and it's not private, but I'm so grateful to have him back. Light and space around us, despite the others crowding. I walk down the white hallway. They are all around me, anxious. But we are calm. Then the front door is open, and the air blows cold on us. I'm at the threshold, stepping onto the hospital porch, and my mom commands, "Hand Julia the baby." And I do. But it is as if I am an orange, an apple, some fruit with skin that a knife has been taken to, cutting. The watered air around me is the seen world. The porch has a few wide steps, as if the hospital was just a house. My aunt is smiling so wide, her smile is all I can see of her face, except her eyes locked down on him. In the world, he belongs to her now.

The Boy with
His Mother Inside Him

Before Mark and Julia leave for the airport, before Tommy leaves us for good, they come to my parents' house, our house, for a couple of hours. We leave the hospital. We all get into one car. I have no memory of the ride, of being in the car with my mother and father, Mark, Julia, and Tommy. It must have been tight—five adults and a baby in one car. It might have been a station wagon. Maybe I was in the backseat. It's as though I disappeared when I gave Tommy away—I can't even see myself.

At our house, we all sit in the living room. There's an open box of doughnuts on the kitchen counter. Mark and Julia have been staying here with my parents and my brother while Tommy and I were in the hospital. He's in my mom's arms when he opens his eyes for the first time. She's the first person he sees. Unless he opened his eyes in the car, after I'd disappeared. Or on the walk into the house. Sometime before the photograph of him looking up at her in sleepy astonishment. My mom smiling, holding him close in her arms. Both of them in the brown rocking chair. He's wearing a soft aqua outfit that covers his feet. A tiny, yellow Winnie-the-Pooh is to the left of his heart. My brother, smiling and newly mustached, holds my son too. Up high, so they're face-to-face. Tommy holds two fingers to his own mouth, looking at my brother.

Someone says, "It's your turn, Kelle." They aren't going to let me go in the car with them to the airport. When Mark and Julia get up to leave, head toward the door that leads into the garage, I'll get up too. I'll walk with them. My mom will say, "No, you're not going. This was your time." After the door shuts, I can hear Tommy crying. It's the first time I've heard him cry since he was born. He's loud. He doesn't stop. The car doors open, slam, slam. He's still crying. It's the last thing I hear.

When someone said, "It's your turn," and handed Tommy to me, I knew he wasn't mine anymore. That they were all watching, uncomfortable smiles, afraid I won't give him back. In a gold chair, I hold him so lightly his head drifts out of my arms, touches the arm of the chair. I was trying to show them I could be trusted. Show them I could let go. Someone gasped, and I thought, this shows I'm no good at this, I can't even hold him, keep him safe. I envied Mark and Julia their parenting classes, the way they held him right, close to their chests, their future.

When Mark and Julia take Tommy away in the car, with my parents, I tell myself they're going to the 7-Eleven. I say it over and over, to give myself a chance to get to my room and lock the door. "They'll be right back. They'll be right back." Only my brother is home, banging on the door. "Are you okay?" he keeps asking. But I won't be able to say anything. Facedown on the carpet, hanging onto the floor. It feels like it's slanting, like the floor is a roof. I'll be screaming without making any noise.

That day, I wore a pink dress with red flowers, as if I were going to a wedding, a party. Not like a mother. More like Isabelle Adjani in *Camille Claudel* when she goes crazy, red lipstick smeared. While we were still together in the gold chair, I tried to play with Tommy's toes through the terry cloth, as if he were an older baby to be entertained, not just born. In the one photo of us together, I hold one of his feet in one hand, the palm of my other hand cups his other leg, his bent knee. He has one arm against me, the other reached out to the side, into air. His head is barely resting on my white cardigan, almost as if he's levitating. But he's at ease with me, nearly asleep in the red flowers.

Constellation

I was afraid I'd hurt him. Before he was born, I was afraid that I would hurt my son. That there was something wrong with me, an evil gene inside my DNA. I didn't always believe this. I had loved babies. When I was a young child, a baby in the room had a magnetic pull on me. In my own baby book, under "Favorite Things," my mother wrote "Babies."

When I was eleven years old, I started babysitting for a neighborhood family. The boy was about eighteen months old. His sister was in first grade. I was fine until the boy cried. I don't remember hitting him so much as I remember the anticipation, and the red mark. I wanted to spank him, but I also wanted to comfort him. I loved being the consoler, that the boy could be soothed by me.

I hated being hit myself. After the first time I spanked the baby, I couldn't wait to do it again. I'd sit on the couch and hope he would cry. Hope I could check on him. Spank him. Comfort him. His sister looked at me once suspiciously. This made me nervous. The baby was born brain-damaged, but no one told me this until much later. The last time I agreed to babysit for this family, it was daytime. The baby was in his high chair, and he'd spilled his milk on the floor. I was going to yell when the doorbell rang, my mother appearing. She'd said, "It's okay, he's just a baby." And she mopped up the milk with a paper towel. I had never seen this before, a spill forgiven, or anything else. Another afternoon, I was in our front yard, and the baby's parents saw me, called me over. They were sitting in lawn chairs in their garage, the baby with them. When I approached, he began to cry. "No, no, we're not going anywhere," the mother said, laughing. As if that was why the baby was crying.

I decided not to sit for them anymore. It was the year Shaken Baby Syndrome was named, a constellation of signs. I'd shaken the baby a little, but I don't remember the shaking being hard. Because my real desire was to spank the baby, and then provide solace. But years later, when I saw a British au pair in court for killing a baby by shaking it, a mother or father charged in the death of a baby shaken, I was shaken, I felt the reprieve. But first I'd imagine the baby in the news in my hands, shaking it, and then the limpness afterwards. I'd imagine standing in court with nothing in my hands. The emptiness where the child had been. This must be what a murderer feels: adrenaline, horror.

I never told anyone what I'd done, but I remember learning from my mother that the neighbor's baby had brain damage. She mentioned it in passing while she washed dishes at the kitchen sink. "It happened at birth," my mom said. But in the moment between hearing the boy had brain damage and learning he'd been born with it, I thought I had caused it. There was a window over the sink that looked out on the house of the family across the street. My mother was a little distracted with the water and dishes, but she raised her head, looked at their house with sympathy.

Though I babysat for many years afterward, I never hurt another child. Ever. Why him? Why the first baby? The boy. A few years later, I babysat for a family with two small children, including a two-and-a-half-year-old boy who had a terrible disease. One fall, and he could bleed to death. His parents were huge, obese. Their cupboards were open—cookies, candy. An array of chocolate. They told me I could eat anything I wanted. Outside was a jungle gym in their backyard with more dirt than grass. I hated going outside with their kids, afraid the baby would make one wrong move. I thought of his blood pooling out, inside his body, outside his veins, me calling the emergency number. But what choice did his parents have? It's not as if they could have afforded to hire a health care worker to watch their kids. They probably went out to a movie or dinner. When I was there, the children were in constant motion, running around the small, dark house. Who would begrudge their parents a few hours to themselves, out of here? I discovered their huge stacks of pornography. In the bathroom, they kept the magazines in a basket. But in their bedroom, the knee-high stacks were against the walls, a barricade of porn. I'd never seen anything like it. Fleetingly, I'd lock myself in the bathroom to study the photos, the positions of the bodies like a game of Twister. The older child banging on the door, and every second I left the baby unattended, he could have an accident. I'd flip the pages, thinking, *Don't fall, don't fall.*

In my early twenties, I went to my parents' new home, which was in the same large development where we'd lived when I was eleven. The baby I'd hit had grown up. He was about fourteen then. He had learning difficulties, and my mother, after teaching first grade all day, was tutoring him. They sat together in my parents' living room, at the round table we'd used every day. Heads bowed together over his paper. He lifted his head and looked at me with a shining smile, almost a crush, as if I were beautiful. I don't even know his name. I don't know how to ask for forgiveness. The baby is in his thirties now.

We'd moved when I turned fourteen. A brief move from Orlando to an army base in El Paso, just the first half of eighth grade. Out there in the desert, I felt even less grounded. There were no neighborhood kids my age. I had one friend from school, but we weren't that close. My role model became the girl in *Go Ask Alice*. Years later, I found out the supposedly true story wasn't true, that the book was written by several adults, not a fifteen-year-old-girl. I wanted to drink like her. The girl in the book felt more real to me than anyone else, her loneliness. I was drawn to the way drugs unlocked and brought her into the world. At the end of the diary is an epilogue that says the girl died from a heroin overdose. I knew I'd have to be careful when I was older, that there would be drugs I wouldn't be able to take.

We'll move from El Paso to a beach in Florida for a few years, another military base. The obese porn collectors lived here. They didn't have alcohol. But the neighbors who called me Helen did. I hadn't corrected them the first time they'd called me the wrong name, and later it became impossible to tell them their mistake. I didn't want to embarrass them. As Helen, I would try not to wake up their child, but I loved to hold her. Her room had a rocker, and all night, I'd rock her until the lights from her parents' car shone in her window as they came up the drive. Some nights, I'd steal their alcohol instead. They had the 1975 Cat Stevens album with the poster of him singing in Hawaii, a lei around his neck. I'd play the record over and over, assessing how much was gone from each of their liquor bottles, where it would least likely be missed. I liked to bring a bottle with me, pour their alcohol, save it for later to drink with my best friend, Sharee. Underage, it was always work to get alcohol outside of a party. Finding someone to buy for us, or trying to pass as older to buy it ourselves. We'd walk across the street to the beach with other kids who lived on the base, Kathy or her band friends. Sit beside the ocean, pass a bottle around. Just the sound of the waves coming in. I never liked drinking alone. It's June 1976, the year of my first alcoholic blackout. I've just turned fifteen.

I'd had my first taste of alcohol the year before, and I'd been drunk, but had never lost my memory. There's a party, and I arrive late. Sharee and Kathy already there. "You need to catch up," Kathy said. She opens a cabinet under the kitchen sink, reaches into a cache of bottles, sets several on the counter. In a tall juice glass, she pours me a drink from seven bottles.

I love the burning, how the drink is nearly undrinkable—a potion that changes me, makes me unafraid. The glow that spreads through my body like the moon on the ocean. Before I black out, I kiss my best friend's boyfriend. A girl runs down the street screaming. Hours later, I come to on my doorstep. It's nearly 2 a.m. Still hot out, humid. A friend of Sharee's has walked me home. Tall, he's something to lean on. His face shines in the heat. The porch light comes on over our heads. My dad opens the front door. Furious.

He's never seen me drunk, but he comes from a family of alcoholics. His mother, some of his siblings, other relatives I don't know at all. A father who beat him. He'd been epileptic as a child, and I had a feeling it was from being hit. The epilepsy vanished when he was older (and the hitting stopped). Another relative had been blind as a child, but gained his sight when he was older. Could blindness and epilepsy be side effects of violence? How the body copes? Alcoholism and abuse seemed tied in my father's family. Many years later, I learn that my dad's father isn't his real father, that there's no blood relation. It's some of my dad's siblings who have the Groom blood—his half brother stabbed to death in a bar fight, half sister disabled by a life of hard drinking—who seemed to have stood little chance of survival. My dad moved us away from his hometown, and we have little contact with almost all of his relatives. We keep our distance. My dad has a nice family, a studious, quiet daughter. That night, when he opens the door and sees me drunk and propped up by a sweaty, disheveled boy, it's as if I've risen up from his city, those people he's fled.

My dad's face so dark, I know I only have a few moments. Deserting the boy on the porch, I run past my mother in her long, high-necked nightgown. She's a tiny, still figure from another century, Victorian, aghast. I hurry down the narrow, unlit hall, hoping to make it to my room before my dad catches me. My brother's bedroom is at the end of the hall, just past mine. His door opens. I shut mine, lock it just before my dad's fist hits it. The impact so loud, I jump as if he'd actually hit me. Breathe out. No matter what, I know not to unlock the door. My brother's voice soft in the background. Sleepy at first, rising in concern. My brother's panicky voice muffled under the sound of my father pounding my door. My father yells, "Let me in. Let me in." I don't. I know he isn't himself. There's a big window in my room. If he makes it in, I'm going out into the night. But after an hour, it's quiet. I lie down. Sleep.

Four years later, when I'm nineteen and pregnant, I'll worry that some gene, some violent tendency has been passed on to me. My dad had somehow been spared both alcoholism and abusiveness. But what if I'm like those people he came from, the alcoholics who never recovered, who hurt their children?

As my pregnancy goes along, my fear lessens that I've inherited some kind of abusive gene. By the time my son is in my arms, I feel like those people who can lift cars off the injured, superhuman. I feel the opposite of harm. I hadn't known what it would feel like. I hadn't known that I would run you down if you tried to harm him, that I would lift a spear, an ax, use the strength of my body, my teeth, nails, to save him. But by then, I'd already decided to give him away.

Godzilla

A truck blares when I swerve into the opposite lane. I grin at my passenger, a man from Kentucky. "Sorry."

"Sure. You know we're on the wrong side of the road?"

"What? Right." I change lanes. He raises his eyebrows and shuffles his feet in the newspapers and bottles on the floor. He watches me out of the corner of his eye. His band had left Orlando last week to go home to Kentucky. For some reason, he's still in town. With no transportation. I'd moved back to Orlando when I turned eighteen, after being placed on academic probation my first semester of college in Massachusetts. My grades had picked up the next semester, but my parents still thought I should come back to Florida and try community college instead. Live at home. Their new house is in the same development I'd lived in as a kid, near Tangerine Avenue. I'll graduate from community college the next month, in April 1982.

"You sure you're okay to drive?"

"Of course, I'm fine." He's staying in one of the motels near the topless bars on the highway. My friend Sophie had spotted him at the bar, recognized him as the singer in a band. She liked the drummer, asked me to go over, find out if he was still around too. He wasn't.

"Damn, I was hoping," she said. It's really the bartender, Bill, whom I want. But he's not there. When I tell Sophie I'm giving the singer a ride, she gets mad. "Then you'll get home at six in the morning, and your parents will be bitching for days. Let him find his own ride."

"I'm taking him." The next morning, when I talk to Sophie on the phone, tell her I spent the night with the singer, she said I was becoming an alcoholic.

"You don't care about yourself anymore," she says. I don't know what she means. Why going home with this guy crossed some boundary between heavy drinking and alcoholism. I'm hurt, and Sophie says she's sorry.

I'd controlled my drinking while I was pregnant—no more than two glasses of wine a night. A magazine article said wine was good for you. In the last six months of my pregnancy, I dated a British architect who had a serious, live-in relationship with a woman in California. Temporarily working in Orlando, he'd met me in the train car restaurant where I worked when I was three months pregnant. Victoria Station. It must have reminded him of home. Pregnant, my drinking stabilized—I couldn't hurt the baby. After work, the British man and I go to dinner some nights, or out for drinks. At his house, we watch old TV shows I've never seen, like *Get Smart*. Once, I sat in his lap, not looking at his face, while he asked why we didn't have to use birth control. I told him I was already pregnant. It seems weird to say how loyal he was to me, this guy who was cheating on his girlfriend. But he'd held me tighter when I said I was pregnant, and he stayed with me even after I began to show. Strangers in bars congratulated him on the baby. The first time, he'd looked surprised, but then he just went with it. Smiling, saying thank you. It was the most normal relationship I'd ever had. That was a year ago.

Since I gave birth, I can't drink enough fast enough. I drink twelve to fourteen shots a night. Beer is too slow. Every night I'm just trying to get somewhere, and the only thing that stops me is passing out or throwing up. There's no reason to stop.

I like the singer's solitariness, the quiet tones of his voice. In the future, when I'm in a recovery meeting, trying not to drink, a girl will say, "Sleeping with someone seemed like a good way of getting to know them." It made sense to me. I'm also attracted to him because he can sing. I've watched him from the floor. But mostly, I'm drunk, and drunk I can't stand to be alone. If he'd been less kind, less welcoming, I'd probably still have gone with him for the distraction and comfort. The company.

I don't know what's happening to my son, especially since he got so sick. No one tells me anything directly. My aunt and uncle tell my parents that Tommy has leukemia, that he's being treated. My parents discuss it. I feel as though I don't have the right to ask questions. As if I'm an embarrassment. A ghost mother. There's no way I can call my aunt and uncle. I'd like to ask, "What is happening? How is he feeling?" He can't be dying. There are so many basic things I don't know. Is he in pain? I offer Kentucky Man a ride home.

In the room, he asks if I want to get high. "All right," I said. We sit on the end of the bed and watch a small black-and-white TV. It crackles. Pot is too calm a drug for me, dull, but it seems unfriendly to turn him down. A gigantic, fake-looking, prehistoric animal chases thousands of tiny Japanese people through the streets of Tokyo. Black-and-white movies make me feel tired and a little bereft, the time before color. As a kid, I'd been sick with asthma a lot, stuck home, watching old movies on television. In front of them, I am convalescent again. He clicks on the table lamp. Some light hits the curtains from a street lamp in the parking lot. The TV's a light too, with snow.

I like that he has very long hair, as if he's arrived from the past. We could be in the past. Before I gave Tommy away. Before he got sick. But we aren't—it's March 1982. I try to stand up, but my muscles don't feel strong enough to lift me an inch, never mind out the door. I've never had pot affect me like this—maybe there's something else in it. I don't ask. It's after two in the morning. I scoot slowly backward across the thin bedspread until I feel my head rest on a pillow. Lift a lukewarm beer from the nightstand. I don't know where it came from. Did I bring it? Take a sip, close my eyes. I'm glad the man is relaxed, glad we're high. Godzilla stomps about—he was scary when they made this movie. It had been just a few years after the United States dropped bombs on Hiroshima and Nagasaki. In a magazine I've seen a woman giving a victim a bath in a round wooden tub. The victim missing limbs from the nuclear air. It might have been birth defects from the blast, the aftereffects. But all I can see is the woman who holds the injured one with tenderness, even the light is tender, yellow on her skin and wood and water. She looks like she's singing, like her song is a bath.

Godzilla's a monster who slept through history, until a bomb was tested in the Pacific Ocean. He woke up, killing tens of thousands. Like a walking atom bomb. Something the people can see. Something the scientist can defeat with his Oxygen Destroyer.

I open my eyes in the dark room. The front door has plastic slats open to the outside. The street light slips in. It can only reach so far. My heart is beating very fast, panicking. The TV sound is down. The picture's too static-y to decipher.

A lot of people think Godzilla breathes fire, like a dragon. It's not fire. He has deadly atomic breath. He breathes radiation. When he does this, his dorsal fins light up. Kentucky Man gets up to put the air conditioner on. We listen to it, clacking. Rackety-clack like cards in the spokes of a bike. I think of my son being old enough for a bike. Remember the tricycle comes first. "Wait," I said, "don't boys get wagons before that?"

I keep having this problem at the train car restaurant where I work too, not knowing at what age things happen. I was a cocktail waitress until I delivered my son, nine months pregnant, and customers would give me extra tips, say things like, "Have a boy for me." My back would hurt. After his birth, when I went back to work, I tried to be a regular waiter. It was more money. But I had to train for it, bussing tables. And the gray dish tubs were so heavy. I'd bleed lifting them. I wasn't myself yet. I'd come back to work after a couple of weeks, too soon. The regulars keep asking me questions. Asking for pictures. I don't even know at what age a baby starts to walk. To eat solid food. To talk. In line at the grocery store, a man behind me watched me open my wallet, saw the one photo I had of my son. He asked, "Is that your little helper?" There was no way to tell the customers, the extra tippers, the man in line behind me, that I'd given my son away to relatives, that he was very, very sick, and that I was not there for him. So, I tried to answer, and my answers weren't right. I remember the confusion on one customer's face.

In the motel room, Kentucky Man looks confused too. "What? Wagons?"

"Yeah, what did you have first?" His eyebrows up again. I'm looking for clues, information about my son.

"When?"

"When you were little." He rubs his index finger along his temple. Brushes his hand across my cheek. He's patient with me.

"Why don't you get some sleep?"

In the brighter morning, the sun comes all the way in, striping the carpet. The carpet is gray, dinge on the sun. Kentucky Man's eyes are closed, and I think he's asleep. I'm in trouble. I hadn't called home. At twenty, still living with my parents, I have to be home by 2 a.m. Or I have to call them with a decent lie fairly early in the evening. I find my keys in the tangle of blanket and bedspread on the floor. Sit next to him on the bed's edge, lean over quietly. Kiss him. "Be careful," he said. I spring back. "No, no." He laughs, pulls me onto his chest. "Not careful of me. I meant be careful driving home."

"Oh. Right. Sure."

Years later, my brother will ask, "Remember when you used to be a groupie?" I'll be in the passenger seat of his minivan, his kids in the backseat. He'll say it like, "Who are you? How do I talk to you?" I could say that I had been a picture of a sister, cut from black paper. That the imprint of skin on my skin means I'm still here. When the man from Kentucky touched me I materialized. I felt alive. How could Sophie expect me to give that up? It was the only thing that connected me to the earth.

That spring in 1982, when my son is fighting leukemia, people close to my family ask me how we're doing. I respond, but it's like reaching into an empty room. As if I'll have to cross that long room first before I can reach my hand out, touch the answer. I say things like, "We're hopeful." All the news I have about him travels to me long-distance: by phone from my aunt and uncle in Massachusetts, filtered through my parents, and then to me. My hair looks like weeds, knotted, as if I spend a lot of time underwater.

The scientist had to kill himself when he killed Godzilla. He did it in a matter of seconds. Godzilla, whose radiation could change who you are just by touch, change your DNA. I don't know much about leukemia yet, but I know it comes from something in the environment that can change your DNA. I know radiation can hurt your DNA. I wonder what changed Tommy's cells to make him sick? What hurt his chromosomes? I think of every X-ray I've had taken for broken bones, lung trouble. I hope it's not my touch that poisoned him. In March 1982, all I can do is poison myself.

Book of Lifesavers

Sometimes the future comes to me in a dream. Or I take a trip forward at night. I don't know how it works. One night in 1989, I go into tomorrow, and I'm on the stairs at the Winter Park health food store with a girl. Her long blond hair between her shoulder blades. I face her, but can't see her face. Outside the dream, I've been working here and at the downtown Orlando store for six years. The store, restaurant, and storeroom are below. From the high point of the stairs you can look down on everyone. At the top of the stairs is the bathroom, and to the right, a glass-fronted office where Mrs. Collins, a former beauty queen who'd gained an enormous amount of weight sits under her white gold crown of hair, braided and wound in a tower. From this height, she would look down on not only the storeroom but the entire store, even the customers pushing the glass door open. Her breasts are so large they are like a shelf for figurines. When she says my name, she replaces the first short "e" with an "a" stretched out for several beats, "Kaaa-Lee." Within the dream, I see she's not there, the glass empty. It must be a weekend. The girl on the stairs lifts her knee, twists it, to show me the cut on her sole, the blood. I help her to the bathroom, but I don't remember the soap and water, just her hair, her bloody foot, helping, and the spot where we stand.

The next day, John the cook comes in. John, who made millet

mashed potatoes for me, my favorite, who circled me when some-one I loved had died, not speaking, just keeping an eye on me at the order desk. John, who once gave me $300 to fly home for a funeral. His mother, Lola, the baker, said the money was John's, John said it was hers. So, Lola said, they decided to give it to me. The day after the dream, John comes into the store with his always tied-back hair, loose, between his shoulder blades. He's been surf-ing. He lifts his foot, shows me the cut on the sole, the blood.

My vision is fine in dreams or traveling at night, but I don't always know what I'm looking at. Like a blind person who is sud-denly given a chance to see. The world is clear, but I don't know the words for it. Evelyn at the downtown store is psychic. I told Evelyn that when I was a child, I'd turn into a book of Lifesav-ers, a library of rolled candy, becoming very small and very large, like an accordion. The expansion was frightening and thrilling on my back in bed or on the floor, feeling as if I was going to fall off, that I'd need to pull back before I dispersed. Before I went in all directions at once. Evelyn said that I'd been expanding my psychic powers. As a child, I called it Big Book, Little Book, told no one. I'd always pull back, but wondered where I'd go if I didn't. Some-times, Evelyn and I worked together with Karen, who said she had psychic powers, that instead of having been a book of Lifesav-ers, she'd been a TV that went from tiny to large and back again. Evelyn said that being together made our power more powerful, fizzing like rain on wires, electrified.

When I was nineteen, after I'd given my son away, months flew by. There was a new year coming, and I went to a party at Sophie's apartment, danced in heels, and fell down tiny steps, broke the bone down the center of my foot. A man with silver hair carried me to his car, drove me home, and brought me inside in his arms, to the easy chair, my very unhappy parents. I lay in the recliner. My dad brought me an ice pack and a quilt; my mom was too mad to approach me. "We'll go to the emergency room tomorrow," he said. Tiredly, he went back to bed. Every hour, my dad got up to put fresh ice in the bag. The next day, the doctor put me in the hospital, scheduled surgery for the following day. He was going to put two pins in my foot.

That's when the strange feelings started.

At four in the morning, a nurse came in to prep my foot for surgery, painted it with bright orange antiseptic. It hung limply. I hadn't been sleeping when the nurse came in. I wasn't able to because I was terrified, and the feeling had been growing steadily all night. I knew it was crazy, but I was sure I was going to die. I wanted to tell someone and have them reassure me that I was being foolish. It felt like a hard truth, like a rock. I kept quiet.

Two nurses came in and lifted me onto a rolling bed, pushed me upstairs to surgery. My doctor came in smiling. I wanted to say good-bye to someone, anyone. He put a plastic band with a picture of Christ on my left wrist. I smiled back at the doctor. When he walked away, I held the picture.

The surgery went fine. When I woke up, I saw a heavy white cast from knee to toe. I was alive. I didn't understand. The rock was still inside me. Every night in the hospital it got bigger and sharper. I felt I had to concentrate on my breathing to keep breathing. I would force air in and out, afraid if I stopped, I'd never get any more. During the day, it was easier. When I got home from the hospital, I'd lie down on my canopy bed at night, under my pink, nubby bedspread, old voile, and close my eyes on the white wall. But as soon as I closed my eyes, my heart beat too fast, panicking. I was afraid if I slept in the dark I would die. So, in the living room, I sat all night in front of the TV, very close so as not to wake anyone, and the people on TV kept me company with their talk, their problems. I slept when my bedroom was full of light. This went on for days, until one day I closed my eyes in the light, and my heart beat too fast again. I couldn't sleep at all. It seemed time to tell someone.

It's New Year's Day, the new year after I gave up Tommy, my father and brother are watching TV, a sports game. Phyllis George is talking, and I'm thinking how lucky she is, to get to live. A few minutes before, I'd tried to tell my family I was dying, but my dad had said, "What?" and watched the TV. I don't know how I phrased it. I may have said I thought I would die from sleeping. It was hard to be coherent. To talk in a bright, bright world of edge and fact. I'm afraid to tell it straight, afraid they'll think I've lost my mind.

The phone rings. My dad breaks away from the football game to answer it. He leans against the breakfast bar. I'm halfway listening. In the bits of conversation, I hear Mark's name, Julia's. My dad's voice breaks. He holds his hand to the side of his head, then his forehead. I stare at him. It sounds as though they're telling him that someone they know in Massachusetts is hurt or sick. I tell myself it's probably his mother's husband—her second or third. He's old. I don't know him, but he'd been hit by a car years ago and has been an invalid ever since. I hope it isn't his mother, Nana Smith. There are so many relatives on my dad's side that I don't know. It could be any of them.

My dad hangs up the phone. He bends his head and closes his eyes. He opens his mouth to speak and closes it again. After a few moments, he looks at the square, white clock on the wall. It's beside the phone.

He said, "That little kid has leukemia." What little kid? A niece, a nephew I don't know? Who? Internal questions to keep my fear down. I stare at my father. He offers no more information. I think, it's not my child, it's not Tommy. He's healthy. He's so healthy, and he's just a baby. Let it be anyone else's. I don't ask out loud.

Maybe my body, my dream, my traveling soul doesn't know

the difference between my son and me. It can see us clearly, like John the cook and the girl in the dream, but it thinks we're the same. In our baby pictures, we are the same child, one black-and-white, one color. Maybe my soul holds up the two pictures, travels between the two babies. But it wasn't a dream, I wasn't asleep. The rock in my chest told me he was dying when I was awake. Maybe it was my son's soul that traveled to me to give me the news, without even the word for Mom, *Ma*, he could say, *Ma*.

The Worst Thing
That Can Happen

It's 1982, the year my son dies, and I sit in a circle with fifteen alcoholic sailors. We're living together for six weeks in the U.S. Navy's alcohol treatment program. I'd been enrolled at the university, but I've dropped all my classes. The sailors are here because their jobs are on the line. I'm in because I'm still young enough to be considered a military dependent. Everything is the washed-out color of the moon, pale and silvery: walls, ceiling, chairs. The sailors don't have to wear their uniforms. Most wear jeans or tan pants. All of them have planed hair, like landing fields. They're all in their twenties to early thirties. When I went into treatment, I know that I lived in a room with a door that opened, but in memory, I see myself behind bars, floor to ceiling. A moon-colored jail.

We're in group therapy. The counselor sitting at the top of our circle has a woven basket in her lap, lots of torn paper, some pens. "I want you to write down the worst thing you've ever done," she says. Even the sailors are scared of the counselor—they call her The Mother of God. She's tall and confident, dark-haired with a big smile, lots of teeth. Her direct stare scrapes at our veneer, our fashioning. Not unkindly. On the first day, she'd laughed in recognition as I'd materialized before her, calling me a sexual child.

The sailors and I are like plates of glass surrounding her. "Write it down, fold your paper, and put it in the basket. No names." No one wants to rehash the worst, to write it down. I hold my piece of paper. It seems too small. The size of a note passed in school.

In group, on my note, I write down the worst thing I've ever done—slapping that baby I cared for in sixth grade. I fold my paper. When the basket is passed to me, the crosshatch in my hands, I drop it in, hand the basket to the man to my right. When the basket reaches the counselor, she sends it around again, each person reaching in to read a note. The first note read aloud describes a nightmare-like scene. I can see it as if it were a movie. A group of adolescent boys hanging another boy, not to kill him, just to terrorize. "Who wrote this one?" the counselor asks. One of the colorless young sailors raises his hand. His hair is sandy. He talks, and I can see the one boy trussed, the way one would tie up an animal before cooking, his head covered, a strong sharp pull around his neck, air below his feet. And then they cut him down. But the boy has died of fear.

"We were under eighteen, so we weren't charged as adults," the sailor says. No one tried for murder.

I don't know what the counselor says to this sailor, what the purpose of this exercise might be, breaking everyone's anonymity. But the basket is passed again. A sailor reads, "I forced my younger brother to give me blow jobs." Everyone flinches.

"Who wrote this?" the counselor asks. My boyfriend raises his hand. I met him here. He's married. But I don't plan on keeping him forever, I just need to touch him so I can stay connected to things. He's short, like a toy sailor. On bus rides to recovery meetings off-base, we sit in the back with a blanket over our knees, whispering, making the other sailors jealous. At night, we time the rounds of the security guard, make out at the front desk. The wood hard on my back like an instruction. But this confession is news. When my boyfriend talks about his note in group, he's a shadow in a house; his brother is another shadow. It makes my stomach tight. He cries. I'm disengaging, as if he's a stranger crying on TV. His brother in the hinterland. Afterward, I'll kiss his criminal mouth.

The basket keeps going. Four men have raped. When my note is read, I'll identify myself. Not that I need to. My note says something like, "I started babysitting when I was eleven years old, and when the baby cried and wouldn't sleep, I slapped him." "That can't be the worst thing," someone says. The entire circle seems to accuse me of lying. I can't tell them how much I wanted the power to hit someone defenseless, how I loved to comfort. I want to say that I wished the child wouldn't cry and sometimes I wished he would. That I was afraid because I liked to shake him and ask insistently, "Do you hear me?" That I'm scared that I wanted to punish and to console him. That I felt needed. The sailors don't think my crime is serious enough. In a way, it's a relief—maybe my crime isn't so bad? But it's too much to explain—the sailors, the counselor—I can't justify to them why this is the worst thing.

I'm still unable to follow the track of what I'd done and don't yet understand the connection between this act and losing my son. I don't understand what I lost because I was afraid that I had a child-abusing gene, that I was programmed in my DNA to raise my hand to hurt another. Afraid of myself. So, I gave Tommy away to people I trusted. In group, I don't see this track; don't understand that I've already been punished.

On my first day in the treatment center, I'd had to see the treatment center doctor. He'd held up the underside of my left arm, scraped raw with keys. A long red raggedness near the city of my wrist, the blue rivers under the surface. As if I'd been trying to unlock myself. "Do you know this is crazy?" the doctor asks. Ribbons in a neat box on each of his shoulders. Black vees on his lower sleeves like birds in flight. I smile at him. It doesn't strike me as crazy; the pain had been a way out when I was locked inside. I'd been at home, my parents' house, the night before I'd checked into the treatment center. No alcohol. There was no way I could go out drinking that night.

When I get out of treatment, I'll come back to this multistory building, I'll ride the elevator up to this floor into my recovery—it's called the Dry Dock meeting. But before that, before I get out of treatment, my boyfriend will graduate, and I'll choose another one: Jason. When Jason first feels my eyes on him, standing in front of me in the bus aisle, he makes the sign of the cross. As if I'm a vampire. He backs away from me. He's levelheaded, dark-haired, mature. He's a higher rank than most of the sailors, used to giving orders. I don't like the way he smells, though—a bitterness comes out of his pores, like the oil of a poisonous plant. When he gets a pass to leave treatment for the weekend, he drinks. But he has to return to us. I find him sitting alone in a dark stairwell of the center. Chastened, but not ruined, broken. I don't remember ever kissing him, but by the end of the month, we're engaged. He says, "No wife of mine is going to wear three earrings in one ear." He says, "You can't meet my friends in those pants." I find it ridiculous that he thinks he can command me, but his certainty is reassuring. I go along with it, let him control me.

I'm going to live in a trailer in Jacksonville, he says, while he goes out to sea. I like the idea of a new life, rooms all to myself. But before the wedding, I drink, fall off the wagon. Jason and I are at a hotel. We need a room. I live at home, and he's in some kind of Navy quarters. On the way to the elevator, we see the sign by the hotel bar: "Free Drinks" it says. "I could get one," I joke.

"Maybe it would be fun," he says. I'm surprised he would say this. I've been sober for two months—six weeks in treatment plus the two weeks since I got out. I haven't been going to meetings very often. When I do go, sometimes I leave early. I tell myself I have to go to the gym and work out. That it's healthy too. I can't just sit in those chairs listening to people. It's hard to be still for the hour of the meeting. I haven't learned to be there yet, my thoughts racing, taking me out the door. I want to go to the bar, drink myself into another state. This is a pattern my life takes over the next two years. Relapsing whenever I put anything else in front of going to meetings. I need to go to meetings every night. Sometimes I need to go twice a day, even three times. But I don't know this yet.

Jason hasn't had a drink since his slip while we were both in rehab. How can he think this is a good idea? The floor feels slanted, walls gray in this drab hotel. I'm not in love. Jason is safe, older—he'll take care of me. I thought he would anyway, but now he's suggesting I drink? Maybe he's feeling confined like me, bored. I don't know what he wants. It occurs to me I don't really know who he is.

I find a rum and Coke in a plastic cup in my hand as we ride the elevator. It's familiar. Jason doesn't get one. The hotel room feels too small. I don't like Jason watching me drink. I hide my cup on the toilet tank in the bathroom. Then go back in there to drink it, secretly. I get tired of him, the dreary room—I want to go out. But there's no way. It's definitely not fun having a drink. My sobriety so new, I don't even have a sense yet of what I've lost. As if the disease itself is buffering me. My drinking doesn't feel calamitous, but I'm unmoored.

My mom plans my wedding. She buys me a white dress. We select wedding invitations bumpy with engraving, mail them out. Restaurant booked for the rehearsal dinner. Two weeks before the wedding, Jason takes the bus down from Jacksonville on a Saturday afternoon. My parents are out of town, and we have sex on my canopy bed. But by 8 p.m., he's asleep, a big man whose body overtakes my single girl bed. So, I leave him a note, say I am taking cookies to a sick friend, and go in search of the man I love:

Bill, Bill, bartender Bill of the beautiful lank hair and many girl-friends. He loves my back, loves when I sit on the kitchen table drinking straight from the bottle. Bill's not happy that I'm getting married, doesn't like the idea of coming to visit me when my husband's at sea. As if he has some moral commitment to marriage, as long as it isn't to him. Bill's not stopping me, not getting down on his knees.

And in the bar tonight, Bill's not even there. I feel the scraped emptiness of the place, cigarette wood, insect chatter, and see his friend, Zappa, named for his Frito Bandito mustache and hair, coffee sad eyes, lazy familiar. There's nothing in my memory until morning when I see the white of a sheet, and Zappa picks up the cup my contacts float in, tosses it out the window, blue blue. I find only one lens in the grass, and have a difficult time driving. By the time I get home, Jason has woken up and is hiding on the porch. "I don't trust you," he says. I cry like a barbarian, an exile. I cry sensationally, a banshee. Jason drives my car to the bus station, and while I am wailing in the passenger seat, a customer from the health food store where I work is in the car beside me. He is so calm in the driver's seat. It's a glimpse of sanity. Startling and clear. In my car, I could be underwater. I could be drowning. I have no idea how to live in that sober world. For a few moments, while our cars are parallel, those worlds appear side by side. I want to be safe, housed in a quiet place where I can think. Jason is unmoved. He phones me from Jacksonville. "I talked to my chaplain. He says I should wait to get married. Until I'm not at sea. I'll be back in six months. We can talk then." The idea of the marriage dies. My parents blame Jason. They say he walked out on me. My wedding dress is a ghost in a closet of coats.

I go back to the Dry Dock meeting. Sit in a chair. Try to stay for the full hour. My treatment counselor always hugs me at the meetings, an enveloping that feels like protection, as though for the moments of her holding I'm safe. My sponsor is a large woman with blond hair and with many sponsees who are all drinking. I can go a day or two without a drink. Something still races through me like adrenaline. I can listen to the other staff person, the man with a brown mustache who smiles at me kindly. Jim. I tell him, "I'm afraid to speak, to stand up." He asks me, "What's the worst thing that can happen?" I hadn't really thought it out. I imagine walking up the aisle to the podium, opening my mouth to tell my story, and then what? My knees buckle. A sharp whiteness explodes, and it's all I can see. I lose my traction on the floor, tilt, fall into the darkness at their feet. I can hear my treatment counselor say, "Well. Then, we'll pick you up."

Seven Works of Mercy

In the spring of 1983, I'm taking classes at the university, majoring in English. My mom gives me money for my classes and books. My parents surprise me with a gift, a $200 electric typewriter to replace my old manual model. I'm grateful for their help but feel guilty for it too. In my creative writing class, a boy with a cloud of black hair writes a story in which the narrator walks across campus, ignored and lonely for what seems like years, until a girl with curly hair blinks black mascara-ed eyelashes at him. "An angel," the narrator says. In class, we could turn in a "private" story, one that wouldn't be workshopped, only seen by the teacher. But the teacher recognized my hair in the boy's story and showed it to me. I hadn't realized I wore so much mascara.

In the story, the boy is seen by the girl, recognized in a way that makes him feel he can trust her, love her. I can be trusted, but not when I drink. It reminds me of police emptying meth labs of plastic cones and tubes, paraphernalia, and the men and women pulled out onto the grass with their dark eyes cuffed—like loving someone who just has to tip over one thing, and everything's on fire.

The boy lives on the water, the opposite coast. School is in the center of the state, so it's a long drive for him. We've been out a few times. I've only been drunk once. We'd gone to the Night Train, when I still worked there. The manager had seen me at the bar. "We're short tonight," he said. "We need you." So I drove the boy back to school, and we had sex in my car in the English Department parking lot. I went to work; he'd gone home.

The boy wants to cook for me, something with curry. I've never had a boyfriend who could cook. He lives with his mother and father, sister. There is going to be a big family wedding reception at a hotel. All his family there, all his friends. I can't remember who is getting married. *I want to take you there and show them how beautiful you are*, he says. The boy stirs at the stove. My vanilla yellow boots are roomy below the knee, as if for some cowboy fabric, the burr and heft of the range.

When pain receptors in your body start to burn from the heat of curry, they release endorphins to comfort you, the one they love most. So some people get addicted, wanting it hotter and hotter. Pain coming from the Latin for *fine, penalty*. There's pain of the nerves, blood vessels, visceral pain from the body's organs, phantom pain, pain of the skin cut open, and extreme sadness in the torso. Receptors at the surface bob free, a path for fast pain and slow. With slow pain, there's a horn to pass, your dorsal, the fish we came from finned inside us, and upward travel. Pain has a gate to get through before your body makes its own opium, endorphins sounding like something that swims.

I don't like curry, but I eat the meal, lit up sitting with the boy. At the wedding party, in the hall where the reception is held, there are bottles. A bowl of alcohol. I drink glass after glass, until I have to lean against the wall. I slide down to the floor. The boy looks concerned, wonders if I'm ill. Why was I falling as if I'd forgotten what the body is for, how it works?

The singer in the band dances with me, looks surprised when his hat floats away on my head. I tell the boy I'm going to the bathroom. But when I drift out the door unafraid, someone says there is a party somewhere, and I find it. In the room is a big bed, and the blanket scratches slightly, though who is in the bed, the room—it is all unclear. I only remember the bubble of noise around me, someone touching me so that I'm not alone, someone choosing me. And then the darkness of the door opening—all the doors the boy must have tried to find me, a hotel of doors.

Later, alone with him, I say, *Baby*. He does love me again before the night is out—a few hours of mercy—before he faces his friends, his family, sister who names me The Dancing Girl. We were back at his house, everyone asleep. I was twisting alone on the couch until I couldn't stand being away from him any longer. Regardless of the noise, the risk of waking his parents, I climb the stairs to his bed. His eyes are open and sharp in a long way, as if even the shape of his eyes has changed. He rises, guides me to the garage, and the darkness of the car. It is the only private place, the only place we can be unheard. Stick shift between us like a planchette for a Ouija board, as if it can answer his questions. He keeps asking, *What were you doing?* I try to tell him about the extreme sadness in my torso. All I can talk about is Tommy. There are men whose hands I can't remember, the touch of their bodies, no physical memory of sex. But when I tell the boy, whose name is Tom, when I tell him about my son, he weeps. He holds me against his body as if he is inside me. And that holding on stays with me, like the painted works of mercy.

The Last Time I Saw Her

There is a last even of last times.
—SAMUEL BECKETT

By the summer of 1983, my drinking is so out of control, Sophie refuses to go out with me. At the bar, I'd tried to trick her. Downing shots while she went to bathroom, drinking vodka disguised in juice. But I always got too drunk, and she had to take care of me. She's had it now. Tired of my blackouts, sweeping up, my sleeping hidden under tables, on the floor, in the parking lot, yard. Drinking, I was safe with Sophie. Without her, anything could happen. No one else knew to protect me. I'm going to meetings off and on. It's the Fourth of July, and I have six days without a drink. It's a good stretch for me. Usually I drink every other day. Sometimes I can go as long as four days. But holidays are trouble—I'm off work, free. And now I'm down to acquaintances who don't know I can't be left on my own, that I'll disappear.

I'm home alone, in the apartment my parents have found for me. Six days of cashiering, of laundry and television, humidity, homework, dirty dishes, dust. I look at the phone on the wall. Run my fingers down the names in my address book. Stop at the names of two sisters who always want to go out. One works in a hair salon and always wears a hat. They're both sort of distant until they get drinking. I call them. We meet at ten o'clock at a new bar. "I'm just drinking beer tonight," I said. "I can't ever drink enough of it to get drunk. I always get too full first." The hat girl says she wants to get drunk. Everyone is cheerful. The waitress brings me a drink that someone has sent over. It's not beer. I drink it—tequila, rum, vodka. Someone else buys me another. When the bar closes, one sister goes home, and the hat girl rides with me to an after-hours bottle club.

Inside the club, an older man tries to pick up the hat girl. He gives us a fifth of both Jack Daniel's and Southern Comfort. They charge for water, so after one glass, I take the square JD bottle and fill my glass halfway, then pour Southern Comfort to the rim. It spills a little. Swallow, take a breath, swallow, breathe, pour it down, pour it down, breathe, pour. I make another drink. I'm going to throw up.

I black out in the toilet stall. Wake up with my face on the dirty tile, other shoes visible in the empty space beneath my stall, at the sinks, the mirrors. It's hard standing up, as if I am lifting another body, downed and waterlogged. In front of the wall mirror, I see a woman with gum, ask for some. Cinnamon, a tiny rectangle, a slight hot burn on my tongue. Her face in the mirror before I go out the door, black out again. The hat girl never sees me leave the bathroom. The doorman doesn't see me leave the bar. Nobody else knows me. The hat girl can't find me in the bar or the parking lot. At five in the morning, she gets a ride home from the older man. Earlier, I'd come to in a house, on the carpet, knees on fire. A blackout is ending. Three strange men stand over me—two dark men who look Middle Eastern and one blond American. I vaguely remember dancing with the blond man.

My knees are red, rug-burned from trying to run when I can't stand up. I'm crawling fast. Someone laughs, moves leisurely, but

I can feel a nervousness in him, that I'll get away. He lets me reach the bedroom door, touch the gold knob, and turn until it stops hard at the same spot, clicking *no* over and over in its shut way, until the man drags me back.

We're in one square room of a suburban home, neighbors asleep next door, the room nearly bare of furniture: dark brown plywood—roach camouflage, corner where the blond man stands, a bed that rattles like a metal bridge. It's very late, near dawn.

The abduction was easy. When I danced with the blond man, he promised a bottle if I'd go home with him to get it. I don't know where the two dark-haired men come from, one of whom drags me back when I try to leave. They speak English, but their accents are from another country. The three men could be students, sharing the house, not caring for anything decorative—just walls, a place to sleep, doors.

No one is setting me free. The men don't like it when I scream. One man says, "I can't come while she's crying." So my mouth is covered, my face, and pressure is applied. They suffocate me until it's quiet.

In the beginning, when I fight, it's like being underwater after a big wave, unable to find which way is up, holding my breath. I push as hard as I can, but the weight is like rocks, heavy furniture, unmoving, as though I'm buried in the lock. I push again, from some other place, as if I'm pushing to be born, shocked it's not enough. The dark the dark of underground. I stop pushing.

My body's empty, lungs like handkerchiefs flat inside my chest. I breathe something that's not air, not struggling. My eyes work. I might be inside the earth or slightly above it—it's a cave, spacious. I can imagine my girl body on the floor of the house, shoulders tight. In the cave a light appears at the edge of my vision, like birds in flight. With a current that pulls me, promising everything, except my body. The need to give in to the pull of the light reminds me of the overwhelming need to push when Tommy was born. For the first time, I'm not hard on the girl body that I see, admiring how she's knit together, torso tanned, white where the bikini top cups her like hands, a string of unsunned skin white around her neck glowing.

Once that body fit in a single gold chair with her brother, white socks on their feet, chair so big it is like a throne. She has a pink coat with gold buttons, and her father had wanted to name her Aurora, the name of the sun rising, so that she would always know how happy he was the day she was born. This is the opposite of dawn. This girl, in this room, could be leaves in the woods, an arm poking out. Grass growing out of her mouth.

Once in a story, a girl was shot, through a door—she'd been dancing outside, announcing a child. In a year, someone in a recovery meeting will say, "I think you would like this story," and hand me a copy of the *Paris Review*. In the story, if you want to live, if you wish it before dying, you can come back. Before she hit the ground, a girl had wanted to live, and so she came back, in another state. When, earlier in the story, the narrator finds the girl in an empty room, cutting herself—blood on her arms, I feel as though I am the girl and the narrator. After the girl in the story dies, it's years before she comes back. When she does, she's a child, and the narrator is still an adult. But they recognize each other, and nothing—not the self-mutilation, or death, or geographical distance, or age—keeps them from being able to see. I know my son isn't lost to me. I know no one is ever lost. But this story is someone else believing that and telling me so. I want to be able to write like this. I'll read the story sitting cross-legged on my canopy bed, weeping, near hysterical, as if I could finally see a world I knew existed. Reading it, I'll start to spin—unable to face any one direction for more than a few moments. Maybe as in the story, when I'm dying, my love for my girl body counts as a wish.

In the house, the three men, unaware that the girl they raped and suffocated has died, are sleeping when I come back from the cave. I died and came back to life. I don't know how long they continued to suffocate me after I lost consciousness from lack of oxygen. How many more minutes it would have taken before I was gone for good. I don't remember coming back. Suddenly it's morning. As if some angel had put his mouth to mine and breathed, like radar echo from birds or rain. Brought my soul back, a blue shadow, into my body. But the girl I'd been is gone.

In meetings, people would talk about the terrible things that haven't happened yet, but can if an alcoholic keeps drinking. I'd thought I would always be able to save myself. I remember a man in meetings who killed another person while in a blackout, who woke up in jail. But I thought those things only happened to other people. When I saw that man, who got out of prison after many years, he was so kind. Always willing to help other alcoholics. At first I didn't know his story, just thought he was one of the successful people who knew how to do the steps. Sometimes I thought he looked down on me for my failure to stay sober. I didn't understand that he could see me because we were the same. When someone would mention the promises—"we are going to know a new freedom and a new happiness"—I could feel a road ahead open up. I believed it was true, but thought that was just for other people too.

I need to get out of this house. I'm in shock, but some part of me is in charge. First, I need clothes. The turquoise shirt with black polka dots is torn up one side, but they never bothered to take it off. No skirt. I put my legs into a pair of Levi's belonging to one of the men. Pull them up. Too big. The man wakes up, complains.

They let me dress. They drive me to my car, but my keys are gone, my purse. Alone, walking, I sing a song from long ago in my head. Gone with my purse is my wallet with the photo of my son, photo of myself as child. I'd kept them side by side—the same face nineteen years apart, mine black-and-white, his in color. My grandmother gave me the photos after he died.

After an hour of walking in the morning heat, the pastel Sunday people speeding by, I pass the train car restaurant where I no longer work. I'd dressed like a dancer there, all the hostesses, cocktail waitresses in black leotards, silky black skirts, slippers. My body like a black lake. A painter once said the body is most beautiful at the joints: the shoulders, neck, elbows, wrists, hips, knees, and ankles—and the back and breasts. Where we're glued together.

Highway grit's inside my sandals. The only person I know in this town is Danny, the father of my child. The sun scratching my eyes makes me want to close them. Mascara smeared down my face in old tears. I want to lie down on the roadside. My skin is pinpricked, stuck. It aches in large, flat areas—my thighs and stomach thud. My back. Inside something taut's abraded, cut like a plum. I haven't been to his house in three years. Not since the early months of my pregnancy when we'd briefly reunited after he'd called. Said he loved me and wanted his parents to adopt my baby. But after three days, I broke it off again—I wasn't in love; I didn't want to be in his grip. I'd started to think that maybe I could keep my baby, raise him myself.

Danny's house is past the train restaurant, on the opposite side of the highway. I'm still not positive I've got the right street, until I see his face at the bedroom window, long hair flat from his pillow, eyes sleepy, watching me walking on his wet grass, as if he's been waiting all this time, expecting me.

Waiting, as though he's got the heightened senses of a cat, even though his brother told me he'd tried to kill himself with Old Grand-Dad and phenobarbital after I broke off the engagement, after I refused to have an abortion, and later refused to give his parents the baby, after I told him it wasn't his child, after I'd tried to run him down in the train restaurant parking lot when he barred my way, pregnant. He'd grabbed my wrist and turned it, like a mean game to see how much I could take, the twisting like a rug burn. I hadn't known what I would do with a baby inside, running to my car. He stood in front of the hood, and I gunned it, imagined him bouncing off. The British architect I'd been dating pulled him out of the way.

This is his parents' house. They are somewhere in these rooms. I met him when I was eighteen. He picked fights. When I first saw him, he was leaning against the wall at the ABC bar, face bloody and swollen. Told me he'd eaten a coral snake, the most deadly, cooked it on the sidewalk as a child. He kept a gun in the glove box, and had lied so long about his age, he forgot how old he was. Cried when he found out he'd lost a year.

Once he drank forty ounces of beer and threatened to shoot my ex who'd worked with me at Dino's Pizza. Once I couldn't see him because I had laundry to do, so he washed my clothes. My brother found him at the kitchen sink, hand-washing my underwear in Ivory Liquid. He'd make dinner for me, vegetarian chili that tasted of can, set a place at the long table in his parents' house; then, he'd sit at one end and watch me eat. When we drank, we pitched fits that stopped only with blood. The breaking of glass would sober him up. But sometimes I'd cut myself anyway, to show him how wrong he'd been, to make it worse. Even sober, it was a lot of riding around in the back of a truck at the beach, or lying flat on my back in his claustrophobic El Camino with poppers, like having sex in a double-wide coffin.

He waves me around to his front door. Lets me in, down the hall to his bedroom. "I've been raped," I say. He sits on his bed.

"You always did hang out with the wrong people," he says. "And you never knew how to drink." His tone suggests I've had a minor car accident. It doesn't occur to me that he's calm because he's got me, he's got me. He says, "I'm in community college. Taking music." He holds a guitar in his hands now, strums it. Since I last saw him our son was born; our son died. "Can I use the bathroom?" "Use my mom's," he says. "It's across the hall." His parents' bedroom is empty, dark even in the day. I'm afraid to take my clothes off in this house, shower. I run water. Splash my face. Brush my teeth with my finger, paste.

Back in his bedroom, he kisses me. "I need a ride home," I say. He kisses me again. I can visualize a metal spoon, a utensil lying on a table, the way it's used but stays contained. I pretend to be silverware. He tries to lift my shirt over my head, but the shirt's fitted, and even torn, resists. He's tugging at it when his dad knocks on the door, comes in, says, "You need to clean the pool." His dad has a cockatoo on his shoulder.

Danny gives me a T-shirt and shorts. I change in the bathroom. We walk through the dark living room to the sliding glass, outside to the pool. His mother will invite me to stay for breakfast. Cheese omelets and bran muffins. I'll know I just have to get through it, so I can be driven home. I'll stare at the daisies on the kitchen curtain and remember a story Danny told me when we were dating. His friends had told him that they'd picked up a girl in a bar the night before. They'd taken her out in one of the boys' four-wheel trucks and raped her. Then they drove her to the middle of Apopka and tossed her naked into the street. It was funny to these boys that, left vulnerable, she might come to more harm. As if she weren't even human.

To clean the pool, Danny drags a vacuum slash broom along the walls, scraping them. The weight of the water makes him work in slow motion. His dogs run in circles around me. I'm trying not to tip over on the white concrete around the pool. It's blinding me, and his dad is saying words I can't understand. I'm nodding, but the bird on his shoulder is too bright, yellow flames coming out of his white head.

Regency

How to survive the violence itself as it's happening, that isn't what I mean. The drive to your skull, the way your bones use all their white hardness. Brain singing with neurons like a city at night. Not the siren of adrenaline shots, the frenzy of the body. It's a gift if you live. You're only so big. A man of a certain size, attacking, and it's like being buried alive.

But I don't mean that physical fight and mental scrabbling. Breathing again. The attacker(s) saying "I just want to be friends." Walking home in someone else's clothes. I don't mean the walk or how you got the clothes or how you found a key to your apartment with your purse gone. I mean when you get home, bed quiet, made. It looked like my bed itself was sleeping. Filmy pink bedspread I'd had since I was a girl, folded like a gown. I was that girl's heavy ghost. I showered, got under the sheets that looked like a desert, waves of pink and tan.

Waking up is panic. You don't want it to be, and it is anyway. The day after I was raped, I had to go to work at the juice bar in the health food store. It's hectic at lunchtime, a long line for sandwiches. I tell the restaurant manager, "I have to leave early, for the doctor's. I've been raped." The manager says, "Okay." Squarish body, tall yellow hairdo. She'll never ask a word about the rape.

I don't have an appointment—didn't schedule the rape a month

47

in advance—but I drive to the military base. At the gate, I show my laminated ID card, and the sailor in his whites waves me in. It's been more than a year since I was in the alcohol treatment center on this base, but I'm still a military dependent. I still go to the Dry Dock meeting, but haven't been able to put any time together. The Queen of Going Back Out. When I'm at that meeting, I just want to breathe the steadiness in. My doctor is in Family Practice. Behind the semicircle desk are two nurses and a receptionist. "I've been raped," I say mechanically. The three women freeze. I feel I should have prepared them. It's like a science fiction show in which I've zapped them to keep them in place while I do some thinking.

When things start moving again, I'm in my doctor's office. I don't know how I got there. He has a sports bag under his desk. From the TV rape movies, I expect an examination. He doesn't examine me. His mouth moves. I say something back. But it's like there's no sound. He picks up a black receiver to phone the police. Before the rape, I'd been drunk, blacked out. I'd tried to remember the street sign, the house where I'd been taken. But even though I'd stared from the car window as I'd been driven away, where I'd been only got brighter and brighter. Until all I saw was glare. I imagine telling the policeman about glare.

My doctor's face is red, shiny. His fingers mess up the part in his straight brown hair. It's easy to do—flyaway baby hair. I stand up, lean over his desk, say "No."

"What do you mean?" he asks. I didn't know. Things were out of order. My doctor's head is like a ball, his whole body has a roly-poly look, even with the gym bag under the desk, the appearance of exercise. "Then what do you want me to do?" he asks. He looks concerned. I hadn't imagined the specifics of the visit, just a sort of medicinal cleansing, a bacteria killer like the red antiseptic you pour on wounds. A foamy green bath of pHisoderm like they gave me to wash with before touching my baby.

I say, "Nothing. It's okay. I'm okay."

This is 1983. Years before, a local bodybuilder, Edward Keaton, finds a drunk girl vomiting and staggering outside JJ Whispers, a club on Lee Road in Winter Park, Florida. This is just down the road from the juice bar where I work. Years before, Keaton and his wife offer the girl a ride home, and she wakes up blindfolded, half-naked, and sick on the couple's apartment floor. For five hours. *Choked into compliance, she escaped in the morning when the Keatons escorted her to her car.* The girl ran home, and her mother called the police. The defense lawyer will say that the girl had *trumped up charges because she was embarrassed about having had lesbian sex.* But the bodybuilder gets sent to prison for life: kidnapping, five counts of sexual battery, two counts of battery, and one count of unlawful interception of oral communication—he'd taped the whole thing. As star witness, saying she'd been ordered to rape the girl, his wife gets five years.

I didn't know a jury would take a drunk girl's word. The Keaton victim's mother saying, *It'll be okay,* and calling the police for her daughter. I could only tell people on the periphery of my life: the restaurant manager. My new roommate, whom my parents had found in the newspaper. They'd moved my things into her apartment, given me the key. My new roommate who works at night shipping packages, backed away from me, my news. The nurses, doctor.

A couple of days after I see my doctor, a religious counselor calls, asks me to come see her. She's in a room of the hospital, in one chair within a big, empty circle of chairs. I sit next to her. It's as if we're surrounded by invisible, quiet people. There are dark, heavy curtains behind us, floor to ceiling, like a stage. Her face is not something I can remember, but she's a nun. In regular clothes. And because she's a nun, I feel I shouldn't talk about the body, use sexual words. My words feel blurry. But I hear her say, "It's not your fault. No matter what you did. It's not your fault." There is a mark across the sky, I want to say. Look up.

I'm supposed to go back, see the nun again. I don't. But when I can't remember what I used to be like, I sit in a car stuck in highway traffic, car lighter on the soft inside of my arm, searing circles that scar white and cratery, perfect little moons, or break a juice glass in the sink, rocks glass on the toilet tank in the stall of a bar's restroom, cutting shallow lines of blood around the moons—and once, forgetting to unroll my long sleeves, set a drink down in front of a customer who pushes herself back, asks, "What happened to you?" and when I say, "Accident," she squints at me, says, " It looks like you've been in a concentration camp." The customer watching me carefully, angry I don't break down, confess, her cramped lips letting me know she doesn't like liars—or, when I find myself in the mirror by surprise, and I don't know this nice girl, her pretty smile; then, I try to play the nun's voice in my head, a song. Her words soothe me even if I can't believe them. It helps to know that someone believes it wasn't my fault.

After the rape, I want our red rocking chair, the scratchy fabric. When I was a child, my mother, who touched me rarely, would take me in her arms after I'd been punished. Though this didn't happen often or seem unusual—we still had corporal punishment in school—it was always humiliating and often my mother's doing, complaining to my father about something I'd done. Afterward, she'd hold me in the red rocking chair, and my body didn't seem distasteful to her then. As if I had to be broken down, almost hopeless, for her to touch me. Or maybe it was that I was so vulnerable then, like a baby. It seemed more like the beginning, when we were one. The chair's been reupholstered, a different color, but she's held me inside. I'd like to show her the lines in my hands, ask if she recognizes me.

I need to be touched in a nonviolent way. As soon as possible. I'd read in *Time* magazine that it takes a woman seven years to heal from a rape. I'm not letting that be taken away too. The pleasure of being touched. I make my own prescription, a plan to counteract the rape.

I have to find someone to have sex with. But first, I have to get drunk. I'm only three days off Antabuse. I'd started the drug to show I was sorry for drinking, that I'd learned my lesson. *Here, I'll swallow this pill, and then I can't drink.* The thing is, Antabuse doesn't prevent you from drinking. It just makes you sick. And while it's "nontoxic," it can also supposedly kill you. If you drink on Antabuse, your body makes more of an acid, a colorless, flammable liquid. A concentration. It was discovered in the 1930s by rubber workers who worked with the substance, and became ill when they went out drinking.

I go off the Antabuse and three nights later, choose Steve, the barback from the train car bar. Blue-eyed, sweet. He was my height, which made him seem like someone from high school, someone still growing. Most of our talk was voiceless, but actual words felt as though they went through walkie-talkies. A pause where the button would be pressed in to listen, speak. He was from somewhere with more humidity, Mississippi slowing his movements. I'd started drinking at the lower bar, downstairs. Shots that made little fires inside. The four long stairs I'd climbed like planks to the upper bar, a boat. No exit from here. Just a wall of glass, fronted by bottles. Steve is behind the bar, standing on the black rubber mat honeycombed with holes. He's washing glasses, smiling. There is probably a list of stages of psychological trauma that I need to pass through. The nun probably knew them. I propel my smile, accept Steve's invitation to his apartment. I lift my glass to my mouth, over and over.

I have to wait until last call, until the lights blink, and then turn on full-strength. I'm allowed to wait at the bar while Steve and the two bartenders and the manager close, bleach molecules in the air, my lungs, cleaning everything. My hair in a thousand curls, maybe more, looks alive.

I abandon my car, the safe thing to do. Steve drives past the grassy lake to Maltese Circle, the Regency. He parks between the white lines. White stones circle an oval of water made turquoise by paint. A fake lake with five flags announcing a period of time, a country ruled by another during the absence of its monarch. His hand touches my hip where I had so recently felt like ash, like a mattress left in a house that burned. That someone saw through an open window in a town where no one lived. Now, under his hand, my hip is only dark.

Drunk on his waterbed, of course I feel sick. The drug still in my body. Hot, my head throbbing, I'm nauseous. The bed is like the ocean, waves high. My stomach feels as if it's biting itself. But so what. I'm in my own body, I'm saying come in. I'm not long gone. Not a bloody thing in a Dumpster, in the muck of construction, ground into the ground of a housing development, a suburb. I'm not under a sidewalk, bikes overhead. *Covered with the shadow of it.*

Naked, dirt flecks off my teeth. My bones feel crooked, but the beaten places lean into him, stop panicking. The vein on the back of one of his hands is a place to go. We won't be together long. In a few days, when I'll pretend he's a real boyfriend, we'll fight, break apart. He'll date a short, happy-looking girl. But at the Regency, my mouth saved from the grave kisses his. Lips pink again, the gift of it, a bow that twirls, unties. Wraps around. I can't really see him anymore in this liquid state that I remember, that lets me reappear.

Night Train

I miss drinking sometimes, the train car bar. It's January 1984. I'm twenty-two years old, nearly six months sober. Living at home with my parents again. Mrs. Collins transferred me to the quiet branch of the health food store, in the Orlando mall downtown. I've never had this much time without a drink before. At Dry Dock, the brown mustache counselor said he loved me. I was forty-four days sober when he said that, not wanting anything. A light around my body. It helps that Sophie's been out of town. I get nervous when the tiny princess girl calls me—anyone I used to drink with makes me nervous. I'm afraid they'll want to go out. I'm enthralled by the accumulation of sober days, counting them. It seems miraculous, the way they add up when for so long I had to drink every other day.

On the days I don't go to school, I work in the store from 10 a.m. to 7 p.m. or 12 to 9 p.m., forty-five hours a week. If I have the earlier shift, after work I drive a few minutes down the highway, to the eight-o'clock recovery meeting on Broadway. If I'm scheduled to close the store, I still go to Broadway. Sometimes the meetings run late, and I can get a few minutes. At the very least, people are still milling around. I can find someone to talk to before I go home. It's good for me to have one place I can rely on, that feels like home. Sometimes, sitting in a meeting, I don't really hear what's being said. I just read the steps numbered on a laminated poster by the front door. If I'm late, and the room's crowded, that's where I sit, squeezed in between people. Safe. It's best if I can get a seat further in, in the middle of things. Otherwise it's too easy to be scared at the end of the meeting, and just rush out the door to my car without talking to anyone. But I don't want to go out drinking again. The release isn't worth that pain, the risk of having other people control me. The worry that if I drink again, I'll die.

There's an inner room where a second meeting is sometimes held. It's good for me to sit there. I have to pass by a lot of people before I get outside, lots of chances to say hello, hug someone. My favorite part is when I get to hold hands with two people at the end of the meeting. Everyone does it. We say a prayer together. I love it. Sometimes the two people whose hands I hold are the only people I touch all day. Except for handing back change at the store, touching someone's palm with my fingertips.

One Saturday night, before a meeting, a little girl comes up to me, the daughter of an alcoholic. She's five. I'm sitting at a round table, talking to a mountainy guy. The little girl and I have crayoned together before, and she's played hide-and-seek with my purse. But this night, she puts her arms around me and is touching my arm, asking, "How did you get your arms to be so soft?" Before she touched me, I could have been a ghost. I could have floated away.

If it's a school day, I go into work later, to close. But sometimes I'm free and can go to the 6 p.m. and the 8 p.m. meetings. The recovery house is at the center of my life. For once, I don't go into bars at all. After meetings, at home, I write until late at night on my new typewriter. I start running again, in the mornings, on the weekend. My mom likes me. She's calmer, softer. I've always loved her, even when she was so hard. At the university, I'm taking a class on the English novel and a writing class.

At 42 days, I did risk drinking. Rachel called. I used to work with her at Dino's Pizza, my first job in Florida, at eighteen. Going out with her was always trouble because it was never just alcohol. She'd always have drugs too, and the mix made things unpredictable, but I agreed to go to a bar. I didn't plan to drink. Luckily, when I arrive at her house at 11 p.m., she's taken Valium with whiskey and is too wasted to do anything. There's a strange, skinny guy in her kitchen. She wants me to go out with him, but I don't. I go home. At 64 days, I go out with the sisters I drank with the night of my abduction, rape, almost-murder. I feel so uncomfortable in the bar with them, not drinking. It feels as if I'm in the wrong place.

At 68 days without a drink, Sophie's back. She calls, suggests we go to Bill's bar. I say okay. Bill there, all in white from a wedding. He said, "I want to know your every move." When I'm 74 days sober, Bill says he loves me. He drinks. Sophie drinks. But neither of them wants anything to do with me if I'm drinking. I'm still going to meetings, but now I'm going to the bar too. Pretty often. When I have 76 days, one of the barbacks said, "You're Bill's girlfriend." But it's never just me. At 80 days, Sophie tells me, "You better just forget him—he left with that Susan girl last night." It's not just Susan either. Now, at nearly 180 days, I still see him once in a while, but go out with other men. He'll never be my boyfriend. At the university, my creative writing teacher tells me that if I don't drink I can be an assistant at a writers' convention in Winter Park. I'd like that.

At work, I draw letters on small white bags, fill them with grain. A mountain of lopsided paper cakes. Sometimes, by mistake, I write Bill's name on the bag, fill it. The front door is bordered by a blood pressure machine. I have to climb onto the plastic seat to turn off the store alarm in the morning, set it at night. I like to wrap the cuff around my arm like a rough hand, tightening.

Uncross my feet. My count so low, I faint if I stand too long in one place. As a child standing in line for the bus, I'd once fallen in the small space between curb and stairs, the feet of other children overhead as if I'd gone underground. This job is a lot of standing—I've learned to lean, sit on the counter.

The store is recessed in a side pocket of the mall. The elderly come here for exercise, walking in twos and threes from Ivey's through Jordan Marsh, a cool chamber. A kind of preparatory tomb. The stores are dying off slowly. Ten years later, I'll be sitting in a Barnes & Noble café built on the demolished mall, and one of my old customers will appear. "This is where the juice bar used to be," he'll say, standing over me in my chair. The juice bar beneath our feet. He comes to my store after playing basketball—I make him a Pep Power in the blender—strawberries, half a banana, wheat germ, protein powder, brewer's yeast, ice. I don't know his name, but in 1986, when I was being transferred permanently from the mall store back to the busier store in Winter Park, I told him I was nervous about going. The day I start at the new store, dizzied by the larger space and crowd, he shows up. Stands in the aisle and smiles at me. I'd seen him one other time outside the store. After I'd finished the Navy's alcohol treatment program, after I'd cheated on Jason. I'd been on the highway, in the passenger seat of my car, Jason driving. I'd been frantic, begging Jason not to call off our wedding. The juice bar guy had been the man who appeared, driving in the car beside me. He was the one who almost embarrassed me into sanity.

Behind the front counter, Pat said, "You could go out with my nephew." We wear matching smocks—thin cotton coats the color of yolk. Next door is a magazine stand, the piano store. How many pianos could they even sell in a day? It looked like zero a year. A luncheonette across the way. Further down is expensive jewelry, wedding rings. The jewel sellers, like the piano salesman, appear to be conserving energy, moving little. Leaning against glass. Sometimes I take a walk, make the mistake of eye contact, and the jewelry sellers latch on. I only make $4.25 an hour. What kind of jewel could I buy?

"He's nice," Pat said. I'd never seen her nephew. I say I'd like to go out with someone nice. A sign missed. Pat arranges it. Dinner. Pat's very short. I decide her nephew must be short too. She also works part-time at a costume store on the highway. I can't imagine it gets much business outside of Halloween. The store is like a warehouse for clowns. Wheels of opaque makeup, little pots of white and black and red. The clothes scratchy and flammable.

A few nights later, at 6:30, when the nephew is on his way to pick me up at my parents' house, Sophie calls. She said, "Bill's moving away." All I can think is *Get out, get out, get out.* I don't want to count anything; I don't want to be counted. This is a moment I know well, the one they talk about in meetings, when I have no defense against the first drink. By now, I've just been going through the motions of sobriety. I'm not calling anyone in recovery. My attendance at meetings is scattershot. I'm a regular again at the bar.

There isn't much time. I'm afraid the nephew will arrive before I can run to my car, drive out of sight. Afraid someone will stop me. It's still light out—too early to go anywhere. Methodically, I drive to the Big C liquor store. Buy two pints, familiar clink; careful of cops I keep my bottle low while I'm driving down the highway. It burns in stages, like an elevator. By seven o'clock, I'm drunk. Drive to the Night Train. It's just one big room. This is where I'd cocktail-waitressed briefly in 1982, almost two years ago.

Three bars. Black vinyl booths with cigarette burns. On the tables, round red glass, beveled, each with a candle inside, a yellow living room. Calm. The band starts at ten. When I worked here, I had trouble counting money in the dark, keeping it wrapped around my fingers all night.

Bill's not busy yet—he's at the door. Kisses my cheek. "Don't charge her," he tells the bouncer. "She doesn't even drink," he says proudly. At first, it's blindfold dark. I sit at the bar, back to the wall. Bill happy at first, friendly. Clatter, clink. It gets busy. I want a drink, but Bill won't serve me. I'm not thinking that I've just lost almost six months sober, definitely not thinking of going to a meeting. I'm thinking of not being lonely. I'm waiting for the fun to start, for Bill to love me.

He laughs scared when I order from the other bartender, but his face is serious with concern. The short glass against my lips, lift my chin. Drink it in front of him. He tries to grab the glass. I giggle. People are calling his name—he's too busy to stop me. I've won—he can only give me nervous glances. I am very drunk, writing on damp cocktail napkins when Susan arrives. She sits down, blond and compact, flirts with Bill.

The light in the empty ladies' room glares like a hospital. No door on the toilet. I smash my glass on the enamel tank. Tiny red bubbles on my right hand. Back on the barstool, I flirt with the guy to my left, hiding the glass. A few nights before I'd dreamed that I saw the date of my death inscribed on a stone: August 6, 1944—age 63. Wondered who I was. The bottom of the glass intact, and I slid the edges into my wrist. Eight little bones in two perfect rows. The bone next to my thumb is a boat; the bone beside the boat is a moon. A bracelet that lets my fingers work. I don't look down. The word for skin used to be grass covering an open place. I quietly set the broken glass on the bar, blood on it. Bill is funny, so predictable with wide eyes, mouth open. The open place is spilling out.

I blacked out. A few months later, Bill says, "You don't even know what happened."

"Tell me." He'll turn away. We'll be back in the other train car bar—he's got his old job back. I won't be drinking, won't drink again. But it's crazy that I'm there, standing that close to him, all the bottles shining. He won't move away after all. He's right there. He tells me I had sex in my car with someone I didn't know. Got a condom from the bouncer. What kind of man has sex with a woman with blood on her hands?

I don't know why I left my car in the parking lot, along with my keys, coat, my tights, panties, purse. I come out of the black-out walking down the highway. Black elfin boots, legs bare to my thighs, my skirt. No idea of time. The all-night Denny's bright, and I go in to use the pay phone to call Bill. But I don't have a dime. Stand in the light looking at the phone. Walk out. Back to the high-way. *How do I find Bill?* It's cold. Even in Florida, January is cold.

This is how girls disappear. Walking until they become dark-ness. A van stops. Someone vanishes.

A car does stop. Window down. The driver has dark hair. "You look like you could use some help," he says. He's older than me, but not old. Maybe thirty. Pale. His car is small, our bucket seats close together. I get in the car. He doesn't ask what's happened. He doesn't ask how I am. "Where do you want to go?" he asks me. I tell him.

"Turn left at the apartment complex . . . Here."

Bill's apartment. The time in between seeing him at the Night Train and now is like a black Polaroid. I don't get out of the car. Bricks in front of us, one on top of another. The people who live here are bricked in. The driver turns his face to mine. He's not in a hurry.

"Are you sure this is where you want to go?" It's so calm in his car. "I can take you somewhere else." But I'm already racing ahead in my thoughts, wanting to see Bill, afraid of what I've done. I thought about asking the driver to take me home, my parents lived less than ten minutes away. But they'd be mad—I'd broken my curfew. How would I explain my car gone, my clothes, purse, the blood?

The dark-haired man in the car had all the time in the world. I could have told him that three years ago, my son had bruises on his legs, but hadn't fallen. That sometimes the past appears right over the present. That I had a ribbon-thin dress like a flag, red with blue inside, and I slept in it after Tommy died. That I almost hadn't given him away. And if I'd kept him, maybe he wouldn't have died. Instead, I say, "Yes." Open the car door.

Bill's front door isn't locked. There are men's bodies sleeping on the carpet in the living room. I bump into them walking to Bill's door, push it open. He's not happy to see me. He runs his hand through his hair. I know it's soft. He won't look at me. "I can't stand to be in the same room as you," he says. I'm a little surprised that he's not at all concerned about the cutting, the blood. But he's not.

"I can't go home now," I said.

"If you're staying, I'm leaving," he said, bending over into his closet, grabbing a gym bag. He leaves. I can't believe it. His room is nothing without him. Even my ribs are distressed at his leaving, rising and falling.

I wade through the bodies on the floor, go into the kitchen. Smash a juice glass in the sink, terrifying one of Bill's sound-asleep roommates. He levitates from the couch like a cartoon. I can't stop giggling at his fear. I giggle back to the bedroom, Bill's room, shut the door. Take a piece of the glass to bed. Glass edge resting on my wrist. But I'm tired. I don't have the energy to die. *I can die in the morning if I still want to.* Then the bedroom door is pushed open. The now-awake roommate comes in. The bed is in the center of the room. He's touching me. "I just want to make you feel good," he said.

"No," I said. "No. No." But for a moment, I wonder if it's possible. Can he make me feel good? Can I feel good? By then, it's too late. I don't seem to be in charge of my body anymore.

Years later, I'll tell something of this story to a woman in a small, windowless room. She's a spiritual therapist who befriends me, who counsels me at no charge in her office. The telling will make me sick to my stomach, the feeling that I am trash—body crumpled, and a hard wall that I bump against. "What if it wasn't you?" the woman will ask me. And sometime after that telling, I'll be in a fancy grocery store that had expanded to include a liquor section, video rentals, a dry cleaner drop-off. At the dry cleaner counter, a girl will be standing in the yellow store light, and I'll think, "What if it was her?" Instantly, the hard wall gives way.

When I imagine it's her he rapes, I know she can't stop the rasping, like sandpaper inside. She's forgotten how to lift her hands. She doesn't think about the broken glass, about using it as a weapon. How she could cut him to make it stop. It's as if her arms are sky. She can see him through a window, and then he's gone. I want to go to her, and say I'm sorry. It's all I can do, even now, not to walk over to her in the store that no longer exists, and touch her face. I've never seen her face—she's in profile, the counter far from the front door, the registers where I stand. She's waiting on a ticket, or her clothes. But if I walked over, she'd turn, look up.

The Monday-morning light is shady. Skirt and angora an inside-out tangle on the floor. I swallow dry. One door away, the bathroom sink drips. I know not to move. If I move, my memory will click in, I'll wake up. Staying very still, I curl up slowly under the quilt, in segments. I could be embroidery. Eyes closed. Sleep.

By noon, the sun brightens. My contacts are dry, sandy bubbles. I want to find my way back to sleep, but it's too late. My hands start trembling first. The shaking won't stop. My skin is stitching, unstitching, needles getting stuck. My ripped wrists burn. The piece of juice glass I broke is on Bill's nightstand. It looks crazy by daylight. Meant for the wastebasket, not skin.

It takes almost an hour to punch seven numbers in a row on

the telephone. I have to take breaks, lie back down. I call my counselor at the Navy treatment center. I can't drink anymore. I can't not drink. I'm on a line between the two. "Help me."

"Will you go to detox?" she asks. I don't know what that is, but I don't care either.

"Yes."

"I couldn't take you back in here, even if I wanted to. But I can get you into another rehab. Can you leave for detox right now?"

"I lost my car. I can call my mom. She'll bring me." I'm not feeling anything as strong as hope. I just want to live. Can't think of anything more than two breaths ahead. But I do want to live—it's as if my bones and blood, my body has taken over.

Mom's teaching first grade, but she leaves work. Finds my car, my clothes, me. Takes me to my counselor on the Navy base, who arranges for me to get into the Gore Street detox. My mom asks, "But what if she doesn't make it?" She looks small. Not even mad.

And my counselor puts her arm around me, the Queen of Going Back Out, says, "You're going to make it, aren't you?" She smiles at me. I feel the warmth of her arm, the astounding confidence in her voice. I nod.

Gore Street

Chain-link fence, metal door like on a submarine—something that would hold under pressure, underwater, fathoms down. There's a kind of foyer—milling ground for the men. A corridor on the far right wall leads to showers, bathrooms, metal lockers that no one uses. Donated clothes spill out of a human-sized door—left open for those without clothes. A staff desk beside the corridor. Across from the desk, a large sleeping room for the men. Their beds seem to reach to the ceiling, bunk on top of bunk, like in the hold of a ship. The far wall opens to the women's side. It's taken days for a space to open up for me—I'm not drunk anymore. It's early February now. For the month I'm here, there's never a bed available for me in the treatment center section, no room with the recovering, sober women. I sleep in the one big room of women's detox with the drunk women like mummies. White sheets bandaging their bodies. It panics me, living with all these people—so many of them, a city of broken people. All of us corralled into this one concrete block building. I have to keep pushing the anxiety down. There's nothing to do but stand it.

The Gore Street detox is more centrally downtown than the recovery house on Broadway. The Navy base treatment center was fancy by comparison. At least on the Navy base, no one was drunk. Gore Street takes anyone. It's so smoky in here. Everyone smokes. Mornings, Nurse hands out juice—fingerpaint purple and black swished in a Dixie cup. With a pill that she says could kill if I drink. I don't tell her I tried it last summer. When I drank three days off Antabuse, the drug still in me. Drank until my skin burned underneath like soft pear flesh cooking in sugar, jam boiling.

We line up. Nurse takes our blood pressure. Therapy is in a yellow room. We cut pictures from magazines, look for messages on the opposite side. One counselor has hair like cold sand, clumped. On my last day, I'll find a note from him on my bed, with his phone number. He'll want me to call, he'll want me even though he knows what's happened. A grainy older man, someone who should know better. Another counselor has long curly hair to her waist—she sits so far away from me, behind her desk, she's like a girl in a painting. I pick out all the colors—red that's more like yellow. Gold from the wood of trees. Linden. We say things back and forth. My vowels are too close together, but I'm upright. The girl counselor and I talk of practicalities. I think I promise good behavior.

When there's no therapy, we're bused to a flea market. I stand in a phone booth breathing, steam up the cold glass. Drop quarters, but no one's ever home. I'm pretty sure no one wants to talk to me. I get Bill on the phone once, but I can hear Susan in the background, asking him mockingly, "Is that your girlfriend?" Behind the booth, the market is a circus—diamond bright, a chaos I can't face. Even behind glass, the phone booth is a kind of privacy, a clear coffin.

One night at dinner it's gravy on meat. I don't eat meat. We sit with the men, and the new woman I'd met was gone. The night before, this woman had held her palms up to me, black thread tucked tight in her wrists. She'd said that the nurse in the emergency room had been mad at her. "There are people out there who

are really sick," the nurse had said, and yanked the needle. Sitting
so close our knees almost touched, looking down at her wrists
held out to me, I didn't touch her arm. There was a TV on in the
background. In another country a wounded angel is carried on
the limbs of trees, like a ladder. Her eyes covered by a bandage.
Head bowed, she can't see that the sea and mountain and sky are
all the same color. How close they are. The new woman spoke
with a sense of accomplishment, as though the story was something that sewed her together. Maybe it did.

After dinner, the AA volunteers arrive with real coffee. We sit
in a folding chair circle, Styrofoam in our hands. A guy sits next
to me, looks at my outfit—yellow T-shirt, tight yellow pants with
zippers up the sides. He says, "You look like a banana." I like the
circle, as if there is something in the center that we are all paying
attention to, that lives inside it.

Lights out at eleven. We're quiet as stones. They let in an old
man. I heard the nurse took his arm, and he went crazy, just getting a pulse. Two guards, old junkies in white, hauled him out
the steel door. He screamed drunkenly, an animal outside. Threw
himself like a sack against the cement walls of our room, an hour
and a half until the police come. I pull the extra blanket up over
my head, breathing the smell of skin in the threads. What object
gave my son comfort? That's a simple question—something easy
to remember—an object he carried, held. Tell me what you saw in
his arms. I gave him blue blankets when he was born, a sky.

The other women in detox are all older. Drunk, knocking into
furniture. They don't speak. In bed, they're unmoving, plunged
somewhere. None of them stays more than a couple of days. After
a week, when someone young comes in, Shanna, she's like a childhood friend. We're the same age. She has the most beautiful handwriting. In meetings, we seem to sit on a white ledge, high up
in the corner of the room, looking down on a yellow light. She's

married, and there's something in the flat way she talks about her husband, what she's done to him to get a drink, that scares me. The calculation. As if nothing can stop her. But how am I any different? She has no children. Always abortions, she said. A girl I'd worked with in the health food store had had two abortions. She was my age, long blond hair, wand body. We worked behind the juice bar, making sandwiches. She told me that one night she got drunk and ran down the street screaming, "I killed my babies." She told me about it as if it was a dream—it caught her by surprise. As if there was a stranger, a mother inside her who broke free. Danny had wanted me to have an abortion. Pressured me. I wouldn't. Then he tried to take my son, and all I could think was how dare you, how dare you.

In detox, by Friday night, I'm alone again. The girl, Shanna, had said, "I can't take it." We'd both cried. She'd left the meeting early, and when I went back to our room, my blue Samsonite had been pulled from under the bed, opened. She'd taken some shirts from me. Once they're gone, I can't remember what clothes I'd had—cotton, long sleeves—I think they were warm. It's still winter, maybe she knew she'd need something extra. In the empty room, with my suitcase flung open on the cot's white sheet, it looks like I'm the one leaving. She's left me her Fourth Step on yellow paper, blue ruled. Her Specific Losses and Insane Behavior, Unsuccessful Attempts to Control, her Preoccupation, Progression.

I hated that the psychiatrist did both the physical and the mental examinations. I wouldn't talk to him until the end. Nicknamed him Igor—tall, lumpy, rectangle-face. A movie monster. He said, "You think that people are trying to feed off of you." That's how I feel about him, but I don't say that. "Anyone who meets you halfway is going to be crushed," he said. When I talk, it's to ask him how to stop that. He says "self-respect." As if I can sort that out on my own, no explanation, no instructions.

In group, we keep cutting out words and pictures from magazines. The counselor says, "Find ones that describe your feelings, desires that you don't tell others." One word I cut out is "reincarnation." The counselor goes through my pictures and words, turns "reincarnation" over. It says "loving" on the other side of the magazine page. The counselor says I've chosen it subliminally. How can I see through paper? Or how can my subconscious see? I think he's just looking for something positive, something to give me hope. I wonder who helped my son after he died. Who lifted him. Could he walk? Could you tell me that, could he walk? I can't ask anyone. But I looked it up. Between a year and eighteen months old, babies become toddlers. At a year and a half, most can walk and some can start to run. Some can walk backward. Sometimes they can take your hand and walk upstairs, but you can't let go. You can't let go. You can't let go. Tommy was fourteen months old when he died. Maybe he could walk from room to room. He could take your hand. At twelve to fifteen months a child can say mama and dada, and at least two more words. Two words. What two words did he say? Years later, a mother will tell me that when she brought her son home from day care, he made signs with his hands—the day care taught the babies sign language to help them say what they didn't have words for. I do think of reincarnation, I do wonder if my son is here somewhere. Sometimes I look for him. He died on May 27, 1982. How long would it take to be reborn? Could any child a year old be him? Evelyn, the mystic who works with me at the store in the Orlando mall, had understood the Big Book, Little Book experience I'd had as a child. Evelyn also said that when someone dies very young, a baby, they came for a specific reason. To make something happen. I don't want to reduce Tommy's life to a reason, an event, not his life as catalyst. But maybe I don't know what Evelyn means. According to her, his reason, what he made happen, is different from yours and mine because it wasn't contained in a long life, an adult life.

One night the fire alarm goes off while we're sleeping. It sounds like the end of the world. My ears still hurt the next day. They make us go outside in the rain, but never find a fire.

When my parents come for private counseling, my mom says that when we lived in Hawaii, when my dad went out to sea for six months at a time, that I'd climb on the bed on the highest floor of the house and scream for thirty minutes or so. Periodically. Just go climb up and scream. "It was so loud, I was afraid the neighbors would think I was ax-murdering her. I could never get her to tell me why she was screaming." My mom said, "I could never make her stop until she was ready." The counselor who would later ask me out said, almost reflexively, "She has a lot of anger." I remembered the climb, but the screaming was like water, something that had its own ending. And there was a war on then. A fucking war. It seems like an appropriate response for a child. I couldn't stand to have someone I loved taken away—to have no choice. To be physically separated from my father. I was already separated by an ocean from my mother's mom, Nana, who had been my primary source of physical affection. Nana who could barely contain herself when I walked toward her—her arms shaking, reaching out— it sounded like bells. But what about my son? Why didn't we ever talk about him in those sessions? I remember when I'd told my mom I was pregnant. Five months. She'd been silent, her magazine in her lap. She'd told my dad when he got home from work. He'd knocked on my bedroom door, and when I opened it, terrified, he'd said, "I just want you to know you're still my princess." Kissed me on the forehead. The next morning, he'd said, "I just have one question, Kelle. What are we going to name the baby?" My parents who got upset if I ran the air conditioner too high or tried to wash a load of clothes or came home late, my parents were calm.

But then I'd started worrying that we'd have to live with them forever. That I'd have to put the baby in day care while I was at school and my parents were at work. Then, at night, while I worked, my parents would need to watch him. How would we get out of that? What if I resented it? What if I took it out on the baby? After the babysitting incident, I worried that I couldn't be trusted with a child, that I might have brutality bred into me, in my genes. I started thinking about adoption. Then at seven months pregnant, near Christmas, I came home from cocktailing at the restaurant, and my mom said Julia and Mark had called. "They said to call no matter how late you get in." I knew they'd been trying for twelve years to have a child. They'd never asked me to phone them before.

In 2008, I'll be in the theater of the artists-in-residence center where I'll be working. It's near the beach, an hour east of Orlando. Victoria, a writer, a mother, who is at the center teaching teenage writers for a couple of weeks, will point to someone near the door, ask, "Is that your son?" I turn around to see who's there.

It's my colleague Nancy's son—a tall young man with dark hair, freckles. He's smiling, laughing. He's in college, studying photography, and that night he'll take pictures of the young writers reading from their work. And for a moment I won't be able to talk. Victoria has two sons. I can tell she's a good mother. She knows what a mother looks like. That she thinks he could be my son, that I could be capable of raising him, makes me wonder who I am. I imagine I look like a kind of old teenager. Undomesticated. She gives me another world where I stand in this same place, in this same body, but am capable of caring for another and keeping him alive. It's one of the nicest things anyone has ever said to me. I turn back to Victoria, shake my head no.

One morning, Sheila arrives at Gore Street. She's at least fifty. Hungover. In the bathroom, she sits in a chair by the sinks in a row. Dips a washcloth in lukewarm water, reaches up slowly.

Washes under her arms, between her legs. It must be hard to get clean like that. She doesn't want a shower. Lifts a can, sprays her hair into thick, sticky curls. One of her eyes is broken, fixed to her right. Her nightgown is thin, filmy. Drags on the dirty tile.

Breakfast is outdated orange juice and powdered eggs. I sit next to Sheila. She said the last time here she met a woman her age who still wanted a drink. "She had money on her. So, we took a cab to her house. Really nice place. Lots of booze. Television. Food." They drank for three days, and then the woman started throwing bottles, and kicked Sheila out. Days later, Sheila said she was making her own way back to Gore Street, but was weak. I don't know where she went the time in between. She walked past a bar, by the Dumpster out back, saw something on the ground. Some boys were circling it slow. She said it was the woman with money, not moving at all. Sheila said she would have gone over, but the woman looked dead. She was afraid the boys would turn on her, so she kept walking, came back here. Why didn't we tell someone? Ask the staff to call the police? For some reason, it seemed like the woman on the ground happened a long time ago.

When I'd first started going to recovery meetings in 1982, almost two years before, there had been a man I liked. I don't remember anything he said, just how he had stood to my left after meetings. His hair was Jesus-long and dark. Heroin and alcohol, I heard. Our greetings were silent—nods, inclination. Like a wall between us when there was no wall. In February 1984, at Gore Street, we were living in the same building: he was in the men's detox, and I was in the women's. Just separate sides of a large space divided by an open doorway. Every morning, I had to walk through the men's area to get my Antabuse and my hair dryer from the attendant behind the main desk. The attendant would say, "Here's your hair blower." They kept it locked up like a weapon, as if I could blow my hair to death.

In 1982 and early 1983, I'd known the man on the other side in those first meetings, standing near the coffee urn before I drank coffee, smoke everywhere, near people who were like friends. It was before I'd found the Broadway meeting. The very first meeting I'd ever attended, in 1982, had been full of senior citizens. I was twenty. They told me I needed young people and suggested a big meeting called Rebose ("Sober" backwards). That's where I met the man I admired. That meeting had been a long drive from my parents' house—in traffic it was a good hour from downtown. But I liked the familiarity of going to the same place. Back then, in that room, it seemed there was a mirror behind the man, with gilt, and a fancy table. In 1982, I could only go a day or two without a drink, the Queen of Going Back Out every other day, but I still went to meetings. We'd gather together at the end, before going out the door. I'd stay with the others to be near him in a casual way, not spook him. His muscles relaxed, but it seemed like he could run at any time. I'd talk to the others, look at him in sips. It seemed as though he mostly saw me from the side. But here at Gore Street in 1984, we're with strangers, both of us still in trouble. He wouldn't be here, two years later, if he weren't having his own problems staying sober.

I'd lived there a month, drawn a coat of arms by the time I saw him standing on the men's side. My coat of arms was made of pictures I drew to describe myself. Four things. One is a shield, or they all are. There was a doorframe between the man and me, but no door. I stood on my side. He saw me. I don't remember any words, but we both lit up. Men and women shuffled between us. Heads down. Even though we were inside, it was like a plaza in a foreign land. His smile long-distance, but it felt like arms around me. Here we both were, still struggling, still hoping, and for the day, not using. Seeing him felt like a connection from my past to my future—a bridge to the life I wasn't living yet. I hope that I meant something like that to him too. It was my last day when I spotted him, almost time for me to go. When I walked through the empty doorframe, headed for the steel doors out, he stood in front of me. If we said something then, it could have been another language. It could have been that friend meant refuge. Dear. And also love. It's the personal connection between him and me, and everyone else just trying to keep it together, that helps to give me what I need to stay sober. There's no pretending between us. I don't have to turn him into a boyfriend or some random guy to sleep with. I don't have to use him. Unlike most of the other men in my life, he means something, exchanges something pure with me. I want him to make it. I want everything good for him. There's nothing in my experience to compare with this. And even though we'd never really spoken, just stood in the same circle night after night two years previous, he put his arms around me. I turned my face into his hair, a place to rest. He kissed me. "For luck," he said, before he let me go.

El Paso

Ochre, olive, iron, sand. Weed and thistle. Backyard blown about by wind. At fourteen years old, in my room in El Paso, I could hear the dark outside. There's a desert in the backyard. El Paso is the opposite of every place I've ever lived. No ocean. I'd never lived so far inland before. Being so far away from the coast makes me feel as if I'm holding my breath, as if I'm suffocating. It helps me to look at a photograph of the ocean, to stare at it until I'm inside. Like a book.

My parents came west before we did, making a home for us while my brother and I spent the summer on Cape Cod with my maternal grandparents. Almost every summer, no matter where I live, I return to them. Stay at least a month, sometimes longer. At their house I know I'm loved no matter what. There are lots of barbecues with family members I see only in summer. Sometimes a relative will see me, standing in the yard, say a few words, make me laugh.

That summer on the Cape, when someone would notice me standing in the grass, speak just to me, I came into focus. Materialized. Someone used to call me cloud girl. Someone called me ocean girl. Summers, I spent hours in the sea every day, voices calling me in to dry off, to eat something, go home. When I let go, the ocean carries me. Floating on my back, I listen to its quiet, blue voice. Underwater, no one can reach me.

I didn't speak much in adult company. Unless someone spoke to me, I didn't seem to exist in that world. My responses were always a stumble, but I was so glad to be spoken to directly, to appear in between disappearing.

Even as an adult, even sober, I often feel invisible. In 1999, when I get a job working for an opera company, I meet Pauline at a morning get-together for people who work at Central Florida arts organizations. She's leaning on the back of an auditorium seat and laughing. Her face is bright, there's a crowd around her. When it's time to pair up on a task, Pauline sees me. I can feel myself appearing before her, becoming more solid. She chooses me.

She invites me to the place where she works—a center for grieving children. It's selfish and secret, really, my going to visit. I want to know how to grieve.

The center is a three-story house with lots of wood-floored rooms. The offices seem as though they're in bedrooms of the house, as if you could take a nap in between typing. Pauline introduces me to the staff; then the two of us go into what would have been the living room—now a reception area. She's going to play a video to show me what the grief sessions are like. It's quiet. We're sitting on two separate couches, the TV screen to my right, against the glass wall.

It's only children in the video, in a circle. The camera focuses on one child talking. Then another child. Before I sat down to watch, I'd been shaking hands, smiling, I'd been a colleague and an arts professional—"I'm interested in volunteering," I'd said. The director had smiled, a short woman with a meticulous hairstyle piled high, her suit a pastel casing—she reminded me of Easter candy. There is period of training required to volunteer. It seems manageable to me.

But sitting alone with Pauline, I hear the first child in the video begin to speak about the person she loves who died. When the child speaks in a calm, slow voice, I know she knows the person isn't coming back. That the only thing left to do is to sit in the circle and talk. I imagine what must have come before that—the blow that quieted her. Her words erase all the architecture I've arranged inside. Without my realizing it. So that when the second child speaks, I can't lean against a wall, find a room to hide inside. Pauline sees it coming, reaches for the tissues. But I'm pulling them out of the box like endless white scarves in a magic trick. The living room is like a roundabout—I can't see where to go. I would run to the bathroom, the front door, but I'm revolving. My face hot and red, everything blurs. I just want to leave, to never see this place again, nor Pauline who now sits on the edge of her couch. But she doesn't try to make me stop, and her quiet waiting gives my breathing time to regulate, shame burning less.

"Would you like to see other rooms?" Pauline asks. I appreciate that she acts as though I'm calm enough to walk around. Pauline continues the tour. We walk through one of the doorless doors into a room of dress-up clothes, sand trays, toys. She said that the volunteers are taught to notice what the child is doing and say it out loud. Things like, I see you're wearing a purple hat, or I see you're playing with two cowboys. She said it's what a child wants most, that noticing. I don't know if Pauline told me this story or if it was in the video: a boy filling plastic cups until they brim with water in a tub, using great care, as if he's carrying hot coffee across a crowded room, scrutinizing drops, watching the fill and pour, over and over. Someone could say something like, "You're filling up the orange cup." He had scalded his baby sister in a bathtub. But now I can't remember the sister, not if she lived or died. I can only see the boy trying to get it right and save her. In the room I see an empty bathtub, but there wasn't one there. In the room I see the boy.

When Pauline walks me to my car, I lean against it for a second, steady myself on a familiar object. She asks if I'll come to her house for dinner, with her and her husband and her husband's brother. Later I'll tell her, "I couldn't believe you'd ask me to your house after I broke down like that."

"That's when I decided I liked you," she said.

Her noticing. In 2009, working at the artists-in-residence center, I see a child dancing alone in the amphitheater. She's asking, "Are you watching, are you watching?" Not moving again until her father standing nearby nods yes.

El Paso is where I begin to speak up for myself. Cut off from the coast, from a beach within walking distance, I'm lonelier than I've ever been. Here, someone will demand to hear from me and won't back off. In the square yellowed rooms of the military hospital on the base. A couch for waiting our turn. Some ailment I can't recall. Army all around. My mother sits beside me with her index cards penciled with things she doesn't want to forget. On the hospital wall is a poster for birth control. A thrill—that here I can leave childhood soon, be free. But I'm only in eighth grade. I imagine sex as a kind of marriage, a whiteness.

Called by my last name, "Groom," and my mother and I stand, walk into an office. I am south of the doctor, or north. The doctor in the middle, my mother facing him. I am in another quadrant. Once a poet said she thought it was strange we had two eyes, a mouth. I know what she meant, the mouth could be a wound, a petal cut open. The dark a kind of bleeding.

The doctor asked what was wrong with me, and my mother tells him. He asks me, "How do you feel?" and my mother answers him again. I remember his turning to face me, to look in my face, his saying, "No, I want to hear it from Kelle." If I could play an instrument, I would breathe into it for him, the mouthpiece on my lips, embouchure. The mouth of a river.

I wanted to tell him that someone else always did everything better than me. My mother especially. I wasn't allowed to use the kitchen or cook; I never washed a dish; the washer and dryer were off limits; I never cleaned anything. I lacked most practical living skills. White index cards with instructions littered the house, like "Do Not Touch" scotch-taped to the air conditioner. School was mine, books. Silence. I look at the doctor, his face that I can't remember—the warm color, he wasn't old. Sitting on his round silver seat, having rolled it to face me, skating to me. I feel thrilled again. That isn't what he meant. My voice so far back, so unexercised.

I don't know if I tell him anything, some stumbling awkward collection of words, or if I defer to my mother. But he'd asked me, my voice is the one he wants, irreplaceable. Inarticulate. It didn't matter, the definition of who is best, who is most competent— whatever that is, it isn't me. Right then, skill doesn't determine who gets to talk. "I want to hear it from Kelle." A spiraling inside my chest, low, below my heart, and upward, a dust storm, some energy headed toward my throat, my mouth.

He's a military doctor, efficient, detached, fairly cold. I feel like something on a slide, a slab, when he looks at my body. But he knows it's wrong to have another speak for me, at fourteen. At least he knows I have information about myself.

I don't want to talk about them, all their talking around me, my circling down into a book in my lap. Going into that world, with the whirl of my family around me. The yellow pencil on the round kitchen table. And I don't feel I have the power to pick it up. Sitting in the chair staring at it, unable to reach out. As if someone else has to hand it to me. The pencil could be across a river. I could be a cloud. An indicator for silence. Here are the cloud forests: a dinner at a long table with the family I saw during the summers. Lining each side. Someone speaks to me directly, asks a question from the other side of the table. The surprise of it opening my mouth. But no words come out. It's different being asked to speak if I'm unaccompanied—even if I stumble, I can't abdicate completely. But here I'm surrounded. A relative says, "Kelle doesn't like to talk; we talk for her." And she answers the person's question. There is a little laughter, as if this was cute, rather than a sickness. The person's question is probably if I like school or how old I am, and those are questions others can answer. But when another person speaks for me, it isn't just relief I feel, it's a falling backward into darkness, as if I'm a portrait, and they're the living.

After Tommy died, when I was trying not to drink and failing, I starting going to a new meeting at a church in a quiet neighborhood, St. Richard's. A big meeting with lots of people my age, young. Afterward, outside on a sidewalk or road, I walk with someone older who teaches some kind of class. He said, "You have no social skills." He said it like "You have no clothes." I want to protest. I think he means that I can acquire them, like learning to multiply, divide. But he looks at me like the El Paso doctor did, like something on a slide. The coldness makes it impossible to ask him a question, to ask for help. I have the sense that it would involve ropes and climbing, group activities with everyone clamoring for notice, to be seen. Competition. When I go back to drinking again, I can speak. The fear unlocked. When I drink, I need people and don't hide it—it feels as if I'm joining the living, speaking. In El Paso, there are sky islands in the mountains above the desert—so isolated they make their own world. We drive out of there in snow, a camper chained to the back of the station wagon—three days looking out the window at other cars, highway, the caverns I'd never seen—and when we get to Florida, fling the doors open on another military base, it's warm. We're near the sea. I can breathe again. All I want to do is get into the ocean. I'm thirsty for the salt. It's like coming back from an alien planet where even the main attractions are underground like graves—stalactites, water made of rock.

In July 1965, I was the flower girl at the wedding of my mother's brother on the Cape. I had just turned four. My mother drove me to Boston and bought me a beautiful blue dress that touched the floor, spilling out in waves; I wore the ocean in the shape of a girl. When I walked alone down the church aisle, my dress carried me. It was like coming home to the ocean after those months in the desert—I felt like myself. Everyone turned to see. What Pauline had said a child wants most. It means I'm here.

When the doctor in El Paso had turned to me when I was fourteen years old, asked me to speak, I'd started to realize that my voice could matter in the world of adults. That I didn't have to be powerless and dependent. An energy had spiraled up, but it wasn't something I knew how to do on my own. I felt amorphous, like a cloud or the ocean. At home, in school, with relatives, my passivity seemed a good thing. I was no trouble. But five years later, when I'm pregnant, I won't tell anyone my fears about hurting my son; when he's dying, I won't be able to call my aunt and uncle and ask to see him, or even ask if I can go to the funeral. Even later, when I'm researching the city where my son lived, concerned about environmental hazards and any possible link to his leukemia, I'll be quiet in my asking. Almost apologetic. In El Paso, for the first time, I had tried to speak up for myself.

Sometimes I wonder if it wasn't a city that killed my son, or even my giving him away. I wonder if what killed him was my silence. All that falling backward into myself, unable to face anger, annoyance. Unable to try. Here, take it, my voice, my life, my child, here, take it.

Space City

My family moved from El Paso to a Florida beach town in 1975. I enrolled at the junior high. Luckily, a few kids my age lived on the base. A little circle of girls to hang out with.

It was still warm enough in the dark to swim naked in the ocean. A ravenous sea bird looks no different at night. No moon. There would be reports at school, but who cared. We were in the water. In daylight, someone is always trying to catch and tie you, rope circling overhead. A wave folds back on my chest like a lapel. I'm small enough to be held in the hand of the ocean, so the ocean holds me. Laughter just a way to orient ourselves in the dark, a jubilant echolocation. No one had yet aimed a knife at me, diagrammed an entrance. My grandmother said the salt water could heal anything. I never went so far that I couldn't come back, the ocean full of crosses. Beneath the waves there is only one song.

We live on a barrier island, surrounded by river and ocean, floating—the only way off is a bridge. Some nights we stand beside the baseball diamond built between our streets. The yellow vapor lights make the field like day. The boring game, the boys in uniforms. The stadium is something to climb, boards wobbly. Below, the women's bathroom is a cave engraved with drawings. Four girls and a bottle. A boy must have given it to us, someone's older boyfriend. It's just beer, but I've never had alcohol. I'm afraid of losing control. So when it's my turn, I pretend, hold the bottle between my lips, lean back, and block the bitter liquid with my tongue. "You just took a sip," someone says, suspicious that I'm not participating equally in the beer drinking. It's supposed to be exciting. I think I take the bottle back just to please whoever spoke. Lean back, block. I'm afraid if I don't watch out, I'll climb to the top of a house, jump off. Die in an aerial display. I know what happened to the girl in *Go Ask Alice*. But I don't know the difference between acid and alcohol—I don't know what anything can do.

In French class, Sharee chooses me as her friend. She gives me Victor Hugo's poem, the easy one, in a competition for ninth graders, held at a university on another coast. She takes the harder one, for tenth graders, lets me get the ribbon. We are *l'école numéro huit*. Together, we climb a statue of a man, fling our arms out. Sometimes we just sit in the grass at night. Once when it's getting dark, she says, "Your teeth are so white." Next door is a boy we don't like much. Not actively, he just loiters on the periphery in too-short running shorts, falling into view like some kind of pale shellfish. He has a party one night, the boys with motorcycles invited. They are all brothers, ranging from men in their twenties to boys younger than me. The night of the party, Sharee has to babysit at a neighbor's house. I keep her company there.

"You should still go," she said. I didn't really want to. We find a copy of *Butterfield 8* in a wooden drawer—I borrow it. "You'll have to have a drink first." I've never had a drink. But it makes sense the way she explains it, getting ready for the party. It isn't like I'm not curious. The kitchen is white. Sharee opens cabinets, finds a bottle of rum. "I can make a rum and Coke," she said, gets a can from the refrigerator. I'm impressed that she knows how to do this. But she won't drink with me, because of the babysitting. She takes the responsibility for kids seriously. I will too, when I get the babysitting job with the people who call me Helen, who have the Cat Stevens album—I'll steal their alcohol, but won't drink it while I'm working. But I'll learn that really that's because I don't like to drink alone.

Sharee hands the drink to me—it tastes like very cold Coke. The thick transparent glass is like a piece of ice against my lips, something I can bite. "Maybe you should drink another one," she said. I didn't really feel very different, not party-ready. She makes me another. I drink it. Both drinks hit at once. My chest radiates, a sun inside. I leave for the party, a few houses down the sidewalk. Speak to one of the older motorcycle brothers. He sits hunched over on his bike, as if the air is too heavy. Only his head lifted up like a snake. He has to raise his eyes to see me. Though he is one of the friendlier brothers, he isn't attractive. Less raw than the others, he pouts about some problem that could prevent all the brothers from attending the party—some indignation one brother has suffered. The pouting biker has beer with him, and he's going to leave with it, his trail of siblings. "Stay," I said. It's 1976. I'm fifteen now. Counseling him. Sharee's neighbor inside the house, still wearing his wretched shorts. There's a beer bottle in my hand. And then we're all in the house, and drinking is the only thing that made it—or me—interesting.

Drinking is easier than I'd imagined, less dramatic. I feel myself cohere around a radioactive center, my arms reaching out like bright flowers. Where I end blurs. When I climb the stairs after the neighbor to see some drawing, and he kisses me—this boy I'd mocked for falling out of his shorts—it is brand new, this kind of wanting from another person. The pressure of his body alongside me, like matching sarcophagi. Though I don't like him much or even have anything to say to him, I feel powerful in a way I never have before, with his body wanting mine. There is no way in, I'm only on display. Ornamental. Sharee and I have discussed this.

We've decided that we have to be seventeen before we have sex. I'm not sure I would have thought of that on my own, but now it's a pact. He's all over me like a din of insects. And where he touches me, I appear—my mouth, my hand, arm, breast beneath my bra, T-shirt—like when someone finds a new piece of land and names each part, the naming makes a place.

After the party, there is still a little light outside. I walk home with the feeling of his hands on me, pixilating ghost hands. The base quiet, military housing of nearly identical low, concrete homes. Same winding white sidewalk. Almost everyone inside in the heat. That base was known as America's gateway to space. *I Dream of Jeannie* had twirled and blinked down the road, but the Air Force scenes were filmed here. The naming of the town had been marked by an imitation launch with talcum powder and some dynamite. I didn't know any of that, didn't know Wernher von Braun's V-2 missiles had made their way here before I was born. I still wanted to be an archaeologist, still thought it was possible to go to ancient Egypt. Even in pictures, I can feel the ridge of an old brick, dust of Necco wafers on my fingertips. I want to find someone, unbury them. See their lost city broken into pieces and glue it together. Find bones held by sand and heat and hold them. Just me not forgetting you. Hello, I would say when I found them, hello hello from here.

Weapons Department

We stay three years on that beach. Then move to the coast of Spain in 1978. I go to school for a few months in Rota, but they say I've taken all the classes. I've met all the requirements, and don't need another year. So I graduate after eleventh grade and become the secretary of the Weapons Department on the military base, filling in for the actual secretary, who is on vacation. You'd think I'd have seen a weapon or two: M-16s, the makings of a bomb, something kindling, a howitzer, lash or hatchet. It's my first job, the summer I turn seventeen, and the military wants to keep us busy. So, before the school year is out, all the high school students have completed job applications, and I've checked a box that asks if I can type.

During the Vietnam War, my dad had been on a ship at sea, and we'd lived in Hawaii, on Oahu, waiting for him. First in Waipahu, where the ground was red clay, then Honolulu. I was eight. Sitting on the shag carpet in the living room, I wrote my first poems and stories. My mom was a student then, at the University of Hawaii, getting a master's degree in education. When my dad came home from a six-month trip, he brought me my own typewriter from Japan. I'd learned to type.

That summer in Spain, my classmates, among whom I'd felt oversized in hands and feet and conversation, are digging ditches, working in mud and water. They wave to me, suddenly popular, from across a field where they march with shovels like workers under Chairman Mao.

I'd not had one date, no flirtation except hissing on the street, since arriving here. But in Weapons, I'm the only woman among hundreds of men, sailors, the military paying me $1.99 an hour to do very little work—some typing, a boy changes my ribbons and drives me to the Exchange at lunch. There are evaluations to type, each sailor comes to my office to sit in a chair, answer and sign. The most handsome had wanted to become a fireman, but had some medical problem that prevented him from carrying people. The sailors congregate in a room like an auditorium that feels like a store where I can choose. I try so hard to relax, but can't.

At the town pier with my classmates, we buy hash by daylight, the sellers insisting we smoke it right there to be sure it's good. The Sahara in the air making everything grainy. I imagine they're photographing, setting me up for a *Midnight Run* lockup in some underground sewer, saying *let's get the curly-headed one—her hair is too big*, none of the words understandable, like a radio that wouldn't come clear. Even when we're back on the base, in the playground I'm paranoid, unable to let go of the bars, swing. Hash was never my thing—the high so calm compared to drinking. But the girls from school are cold most of the time, except when we go into town to buy, and this is something we can do together. In Spain, I'm not allowed to go anywhere alone. So I'm grateful for the companionship, being outside. On my arrival in Rota, I'd heard cautionary stories of American military kids who'd been caught with hash by the Guardia and imprisoned in the Spanish jail. I was told that unless the families of the imprisoned kids brought food, they didn't eat. When the families got transferred out of the country, the jailed teenagers supposedly got left behind. Though the stories sounded made up, they still scared me. But I was too lonely to stay home. And even less confident—my meager social skills degrading with the move to a new country, new school. There's one beautiful girl, smart and kind, who befriends me. We go running at night. Sometimes she takes me to parties in town, everyone high. It seems rude not to participate. I take the risk. The drug itself seems harmless. Unlike alcohol, it doesn't change my personality.

At work in Weapons, I choose a boy with John Lennon glasses, blue hearts. His smile so calm it's a song poured down my throat, ramshackle chest blanketed. He isn't like the men I'll go out with when I come back to the States, not like the one who'll say he likes women with breasts visible from behind, swelling from the side like cakes, or the nickle-eyed man who'll watch other women on the street, saying he loves how every woman in the city dresses up for him. The boy in Weapons can see me. Though when he and I are together, we're mostly high.

I leave my family in Spain, move to Bridgewater, Massachusetts, for college. Headed toward my son—we're less than three years away from each other.

In Massachusetts, when the boy's letter comes, it's the first time I've seen his handwriting and learn he can't spell, can barely think in ink. Out of uniform, his cords had slung down his hips. Hair too long. An angel dust dealer from a mountain town in Montana, joining the Navy at seventeen, giving up on school. Before I met him, I'd been so lonely for touch that I'd run for miles at night with shin splints just to move through air. His arms, even in memory, were like a coat I could wear.

Sugar Mountain

A friend once told me he couldn't listen to Neil Young songs after hearing gossip that he'd written them underneath the influence of heroin. I'd often wished to be under that influence, but alcohol, cocaine, Qualuudes sent me into guardrails on the highway, and I knew heroin would take the light right out—I'd be a flashlight switched off, sent to live underground. I mean, I tripped waking up. And I still felt instructed by the girl I thought was real in *Go Ask Alice*, the heroin overdose that killed her. Alcohol seemed like something I could measure. The number of drinks countable, or an empty bottle, but heroin seemed uncontrollable, a flood. Though I'm not writing Neil off for finding a way in.

Before Gore Street, I was in love with a man who sang me Neil Young's songs—"Down By the River," "Sugar Mountain." And losing him broke me in a way that pushed me further inside myself. We started going out in 1981, the summer after Tommy was born. The man who could sing showed me the place in his hand where his mother had died, where he thought he saw his own death. When we broke up, I sat on my bed for a long time. Stared at the white wall, wooden closet door. I'd started seeing the Sugar Mountain Man just after he'd separated from his wife. We were together three months. But I'd known him since I worked in the train car restaurant. He'd been the kitchen manager. In 1979, when I'd gone for my interview, I'd opened the back door into the kitchen, stepping in heels onto the black rubber mat on the floor. I was nervous about the interview, and my heels got stuck in the little holes of the mat. I was trying to get unstuck, when I looked up and saw him smiling at me. He had the very pale skin of a Northerner, straight dark hair. He gave me his hand. But I was with Danny, about to get pregnant, and he was about to get married. It'll be two more years before one of the other cooks from the restaurant starts dating me even though he has a serious girlfriend. I like him because he calls me Cosmo Girl and tells me I should be in a magazine. He's companionable. (It's not long after I've given Tommy to my relatives, and I can't stand to be alone.) One night I get very drunk at a party, black out, and the cook panics, doesn't know what to do with me, his girlfriend waiting at home. The Sugar Mountain Man had been at the same party, and had given his friend, the cook, his house keys. So the cook takes me to the empty house and leaves me there.

In the morning, when the Sugar Mountain Man comes home, he finds me in his bed. He's sweet about it, laughing. After I dress, he gives me a glass of juice, plays some music for me. We talk all afternoon, until it's time for me to go to work, bartending at the train car restaurant. He's not working there anymore. I don't have my car, so he's giving me a ride home. My hair an explosion of curls from swimming in a pool at the party, sleeping on it wet— and he gently tries to fit his extra motorcycle helmet on my head. Tries to get strands out of my eyes. Laughing. I tell him to come into the bar, that I'll buy him a beer. He does. I see him almost every night for three months.

Some afternoons, I work my other job at the Merry-Go-Round, a clothing store in the Altamonte mall, about a half hour north of Orlando. The music is terrible, disco, very upbeat. I'm selling clubwear for men and women. I tell the Sugar Mountain Man how the manager tells me I'm not friendly enough with the customers, that I should approach them in a dancing kind of way, as if we're in a club. It's so ridiculous—I can't do it. But the next day, the Sugar Mountain Man comes to see me at work. He's not a shy person, but he's self-contained. Not loud or outgoing. As he enters the store from the dim mall, he starts snapping his fingers and dancing towards me. Not caring what anyone else thinks. Doing it to make me laugh. Once he worked an especially long shift at his new restaurant, and overslept when we were supposed to go out. The next day, he came to the mall with a dozen red roses, said he'd never sleep again. No one had ever given me flowers. When he looked at me, I could tell he thought he was seeing someone beautiful. It made me feel as though I mattered.

He and his wife were about to divorce when she called, told him she was pregnant. There was nothing to do about it. He was angry at everybody. Backtalked a cop, wound up in jail. When I bailed him out, his clothes were sour, his face. We were sour—he couldn't leave her pregnant. So that was that. I went to a party and drank half a bottle of something, six Kamikazes, took part of a Qualuude. I remember a friend repeating to me, "I'm sure he still loves you." When she drove me home, I slipped off the seat, into the dark under her glove compartment. I decided to drop out of community college for the semester, just work all the time.

In the summer of 1981, I worked mornings in a doughnut shop, and some afternoons in the Merry-Go-Round, then in the juice bar next door to it. Later, I worked nights in the Night Train, cocktailing. It was all a lot of standing. Each job had its own outfit: at the Night Train, it was black shorts and suspenders, white shirt, red bow, but at the doughnut store, they kept the uniforms jumbled in a big cardboard box, and you got a choice—tan pants with a pink/tan top, or a dress the color of milky coffee. I chose the dress because I'd always preferred skirts and felt a kinship with

Ann Wilson in her *Rolling Stone* interview when she said skirts were more hygienic.

It was a month before a coworker told me that my dress was really a top. It had seemed awfully short, and I couldn't bend over to get the lower doughnuts—had to curtsy like a princess. Nothing costs much at the doughnut shop, nor was there much to do to impress anyone, so the tips sucked—I'd see a dime and nickle beside an empty coffee cup, and think, *why bother?*

I was offered a raise and a promotion, assistant manager, full-time doughnut work, which seemed surprising since I'd had trouble just getting dressed. Around the corner, almost within sight of the doughnut shop, my boyfriend had sung "Sugar Mountain" in his room, an airless hallway in a tiny house on the side of the road. But the doughnuts at the shop didn't even seem like sugar, dry cake the baked equivalent of a headache—I didn't like coffee either, the heated bad breath, mouths like bitter ovens. Only frosting was appealing, sprinkles and jelly, and the boxes, the way a dozen fit, a large family of doughnuts on their way. So I turned down the entire two hundred and eventually quit.

I'd met Sophie that year too, my drinking friend, when we both worked at the juice bar in the Altamonte mall. In the fall of 1981, we started going out drinking together. Almost every night. By the spring of 1982, when Tommy was dying, she said I didn't care about myself anymore. I wasn't even trying to control my drinking. Stayed at her house a lot, or slept in my car.

Now it's March 1984. I just got out of the Gore Street detox. My parents had come to pick me up. My dad told me that my mom had pounded her fists on the wallpaper in the kitchen, on the little orange teapots, crying, saying, "I can't take her back." But she did. After work, I go to the one bright place on the road that isn't a bar and drink five cups of coffee in the doughnut shop where I'd worked the summer of 1981. The new night baker holds up his index finger to the waitress, telling her to only charge me for one. It's almost Tommy's third birthday. I remember going to a meeting right after he died. Sitting at the folding fake wood table where I never stayed sober more than a day or two, a meeting I once attended fully drunk. I told them I'd been out drinking in the woods, in what looked like another country—a field, trees, no people. I said, "When I came home, they told me my son died." I realized it sounded as though he'd died when I was drinking, but he'd actually died before I went out the door. I wasn't drunk when he died, but the people in the room looked at me as if I had been—a kind of transfixed pity you'd have for a person on fire, not wanting to touch them, grateful it isn't you. An object lesson. Everyone seemed very far away, as if I were talking to them from inside a TV.

I learned to drink coffee in meetings. So nervous, I wanted to sit on my hands, and the white Styrofoam cup gave me something to hold onto. The urn coffee chemically bitter, as though it were brewed from volcanic ash. And I'd read that hot liquids in Styrofoam could turn carcinogenic. But I sipped the coffee like a cocktail, in a way I never drank alcohol. Sipping made the taste manageable, the predominant taste just heat.

The lights in the doughnut shop get brighter and brighter as the waitress keeps filling up my cup. Being back at the shop is kind of like visiting a house I used to live in. I know how the cement felt beneath my feet, the corner in the back room where I'd sit on my break to eat a corn muffin. My feet dangle under the counter. I could spin on the plush round seat. Lately, I've been trying to remember how to walk. I've forgotten what to do with my arms, my facial expressions, my voice. I'm sober almost six weeks. Two weeks out of treatment. I can't just stare at other people walking, so I go to the movies alone, try to see how to behave. I watch *The Hotel New Hampshire*, Frannie getting shoved into a dryer and raped. Her brother carries her home afterward and says, "If someone touches you, and you don't want to be touched, then they haven't touched the you in you." I still can't open a dryer door without thinking about her.

At the health food store, Mrs. Collins had given me a month's leave from work to go into treatment. She'd held my job for me. Now I'm back, working in the Orlando mall location. One of the other clerks, Carey, convinces me to go out with her ex-boyfriend's cousin. Gryf. "He's a little rough around the edges," she says. It's a blind date. We go to a bar. I'm not drinking, but I was still counting days sober.

I don't drink. Gryf and I talk about the beach. He says, "I go to Playalinda. Even though it's a nude beach, and you'd expect to see a lot of fucking, you don't." He doesn't actually say "fucking," instead, he makes a circle with two fingers and puts another finger through it. I don't tell him that I don't expect to see any fucking on the beach. He says, "I work hard, I play hard, and that's a fact." He says it twice, slowly. When he drives me home, and I jump out of the car, he looks surprised. It's disappointing that Carey thinks this is an appropriate guy for me. It makes me wonder how she sees me—how anyone sees me—as though to other people I'm nowhere near who I think I am.

The next night, I'm back at the doughnut shop. The Night Baker says, "I wait every night for you to come in." He says, "You smell like apricots." It's from work—the little vials of scented oils that you apply with a wand. I turn my hand over, lift my wrist up for him. "Skip work tomorrow," he says. "Spend the day, all day, swimming at my house." I can't. I need the money. And I'm not sure about the Night Baker—he's beautiful, but he could be the kind of guy who likes all women. I could just be one of the women he likes. I'm fixating on him anyway. As the compulsion to drink lifts, I'll fixate on anything. It makes me feel dizzy. High on multiple cups of coffee, I go home to write in my bedroom.

After work, the next night, I go to the doughnut shop. "Your next weekday off, you're going to spend swimming with me," he said.

"Oh yeah?" I said. It does seem as though this is just about sex, I mean even the barbaric blind date guy took me somewhere. The Night Baker touches both my arms, casually, but it seems like he has to touch me somewhere. He fastens on my upper arm as if he is going to keep me there. As though he can make me do what he wants.

My name is carved with a heart and some other writing and an arrow into a red vinyl seat at the doughnut shop, the second one over from the cash register. "Kelly" is misspelled, I think. I don't want anyone to catch me trying to read it, so can't get a real good look. The Night Baker goes to court tomorrow to get divorced. He's twenty-eight.

My car breaks down. I don't have the $200 to fix it, so take the bus to work. In Orlando, the buses only work if you live downtown. Here on the outskirts, they run every hour or so. Miss it, and you're stuck for another hour's wait. Without my car, there are no meetings, no doughnut shop. It was easy to think I'd been progressing—almost three months without a drink, until something screws up, and I feel trapped. I head to the end table in my bedroom, grab my keys, and rip the insides of my arms with them. I just want to open a window. Go into the cold air and let it blow this anger out of me. Walk into someplace new. I sit at my desk and start writing. My arm red, with darker red spots. Swollen, bumpy with long ridges. I'm afraid to stop typing. I'm afraid I'll start to die if I do.

Car gets fixed. My parents loan me the money. I go to the doughnut shop and almost cry when there's a pretty girl in the back with the Night Baker. She has a baby. He seems to not want to talk to me around her. She happens to leave just a moment before I do, and the Night Baker follows me out and flirts like crazy. I've kind of had it with him. He says, "I saw you looking at that baby." He doesn't know anything about me really. Doesn't know my baby died. Doesn't know that all I feel when I look at her baby is the emptiness along the inside of my arms where I held my son. The emptiness in the center of my chest where he rested. I did everything I could not to feel that emptiness—still would—short of killing myself.

After that night, I feel nervous in the doughnut shop. Scared of the Night Baker. It feels like panic. He's friendly, but he stops flirting, no comments, no leers. Once, after he'd just been to the beach, he comes up close to me, but one of us veers off. "Come back and see how my sunburn turns to tan." He laughs.

Jeannette at work said, "If you haven't gone out with him yet, then he doesn't want to. He must not like you that much." Inviting me to his pool to swim doesn't count. She's very straightforward. Once when a customer was stealing a piece of frozen liver under her coat, Jeannette just rang up her other items, and said, "These onions will go nicely with that liver." So the customer handed the liver to Jeanette. My other coworkers, Chris and Pat and Stephanie, don't agree with Jeannette's reasoning about the Night Baker. They think he likes me.

It was my three-month sobriety anniversary last night, but they were out of 90-day chips at my home group, so I didn't get one. The poker chips mark the crucial anniversaries of sobriety. The white chip for new people, and for those coming back after drinking— it's a desire chip. For those who want a new way of life. I have a collection of white chips. I surrendered over and over, took it back. But now I'm here again, 90 days sober. The first chip is always white, but meetings use various colors for the other anniversaries. At the meeting on Broadway, the 90-day chip was yellow. I'm calmer in this meeting, safe in the little house where it's held.

Even though they're out of chips, everyone claps for me anyway. I feel pathetic, wanting the poker chip, not getting one. But then, as I'm leaving the meeting, J. gives me his own yellow three-month chip. It's a special one with a message in the center. J. had been sober twelve years, and he has his three-month chip on him. In his pocket. I mean, he's had this chip for almost twelve years, and he still carries it with him. And he gives it to me. I put it in the pocket of my jeans. I like the feel of the ridges around the chip's edge on my fingertips.

At the doughnut shop, the Night Baker walks me outside and tries to kiss me between my car and the Dumpster out back. I'm scared. I'd heard him talking to a friend in the shop about buying a diamond, so he must have had someone he's buying it for. Something inside me had dropped, a weight down to the floor of me. A diamond. In the two months since I've left treatment, I've gotten okay with walking, and have figured out what to do with my arms. I can make a little conversation. But this is an unexpected humiliation. I am too lonely to see straight. And then when this guy kisses me, he'd been meaning it as a little kiss. Some introductory thing. Which I had very little sober experience with—the opposite of drunken kissing. I try too hard, blotting out the diamond. The Night Baker said, "Slow down, I'm not going to hurt you." He seems to recognize my aggressiveness as anxiety. I have the feeling of falling back into the open window of a car. The feeling I had as a child when someone else would speak for me. Falling into darkness. I don't know how to get back out. The Night Baker said, "I won't be working Monday—come in Tuesday."

The final night I go to the doughnut shop, the Night Baker said, "I had a bad day. But it's all right now because you're here." He hugs me, kisses me a little. "I must have just missed calling you today," he said, "I didn't set my clock back right." He wants me to come to his house to fool around. His words exactly. "I see you don't trust me," he said. Shit, what's there to trust in something as blunt as that? The pretty girl comes in. Maybe the diamond is for her. She gathers the waitresses around her, laughs, walks the shop end to end, marking her ground.

I miss the long gone Sugar Mountain Man, his way of seeing me. His beautiful songs. But the Night Baker, Bill, drinking—they seem like ways of falling back. I remember when I'd looked at a pencil on a table and felt powerless. As though I couldn't pick it up. That passivity. I'd need someone else to hand it to me. That summer, after work and meetings, I go home and read, write. It's so hot in my bedroom, I have to write in just my underwear. To use the typewriter, I have to unplug the fan because there are only two sockets, and one is for my lamp. Without the lamp, I can't see to type. So I sit there night after night, slick with sweat—humming from drinking instant coffee, urn coffee, high as I can get without drugs. I stay up until morning to write, to plead to the paper as if it is a telephone, a telegraph, a telegram, as if all I have to do is write, and I'll be heard.

Broadway

Since I got out of treatment in February 1984, my transfer to the less busy health food store has been made semipermanent. I think Mrs. Collins is trying to give me a break with the slower pace. So every night, I can just drive down the highway to the recovery meeting house on Broadway. Around back, the stairs lead to a door, a counter where I can buy a cup of coffee for a quarter. Clouds of smoke in the hallway lead to three rooms with chairs. If the main room's packed, someone will volunteer to lead another meeting in one of the other rooms. I have asthma—the best I can do is not sit next to a smoker. But it's hard to tell, you have to take one of the few empty seats. And then your neighbor lights up. Black ashtrays like clawed hands on the table, carpet.

Before it's my turn to speak, I always panic. Maybe seven people before me, my heart's racing. If I'm lucky, I can just say, "My name's Kelle. I'm an alcoholic, and I pass." Once I try to talk, but can't. Wind up crying, and the chair lets me cry for a couple of minutes, as if those were words. Moves on to the next person.

Mike smokes. He never seems nervous when he speaks in meetings. Tall, bony, red-haired, sitting against the wall or at the table. I could swear a light opens up over his head, pours down. I could hear him. Other people saw it too. After meetings, people crowd him. But I stick it out. I don't have anywhere to go. Eventually the coffee counter guy will turn the lights out, say, "It's time to go." Mike and I will be on the porch or the sidewalk, and we'll talk. Or we'll go to the International House of Pancakes for hours and talk. Mostly I talk. Tell him everything I can't say. Night after night. I know it's selfish, but I want to live. I need him.

One night, the last thing he says to me is "Don't work too hard tomorrow. Do what you have to. But don't work hard."

The next night he's not in the house on Broadway.

T. says, "Have you heard what happened to Mike?"

"To Mike?" I have to tug his name out, as if I can keep his name safe inside me. The night before he'd told me he was worried. He had some work lined up, but had never done this kind of thing before. Cutting limbs off trees. I didn't know that would mean climbing high, that one of the limbs would fall on him. The chain saw fell on his neck, and he fell. Broke both arms, smashed his face. That night he was in a critical care unit, waiting for space in intensive care. Then surgery, pins in his elbows and wrists, his temples, mouth wired back together, a month in the hospital. It was as if his face slipped off, down. As if a face is a mask that can come loose. Mouth a mess. Mouth that T. kissed on her way out of the meeting last night. I watched their lips meet perfectly, and T. saying she liked to kiss a lot, that she liked to kiss more than anyone she knew, that she called people up just to kiss them across the phone.

For months Mike has pins in his skull, mouth wired shut, both arms in casts. He has to drink all his food through a straw. No job, no insurance, no family. Just us. People take him in. Sometimes I pick him up, and we go to a meeting. I can see he doesn't want to go home and stare at four walls, wait for his bones to knit. So we go for coffee. Mike can calm me down, all that anxiety thumping in me, just with a look. Once, he said, "I'm more honest talking with you than with myself because I wouldn't want to tell you something that wasn't true."

Saturday night I picked him up, took him to the New England meeting. He's so tall, bony, with so many broken parts, I'm nervous helping him out of my small car. The pins in his head held in place with a kind of Frankenstein brace. I don't want to jostle him, hurt him. He liked the meeting. I'm not used to helping anyone. Usually it seems as though anyone else would be better suited—whatever the task. But Mike actually needs me. There's a place with nobody in it. I'd made him two Pep Powers at work, packed the protein shakes into a bag for him. He said they were even better than coffee. I gave him a birthday card. He's thirty-two. The humidity makes his healing bones ache.

Since he fell, I've been alone more. Not talking. At work, I cracked inside, went in the bathroom. Hyperventilated. I think I need to ask someone to be my sponsor. When I ask M.J., she says she'll help me do my fourth step. She says, "It's nice to see you smile."

At home, I lay my head down on my humming typewriter, try to pick up some energy. That night I dream that a coworker who doesn't like me gave me a quart of Wild Turkey. In the dream I drink three inches straight from the bottle.

At work, Carey comes over from the Winter Park store. We act out the diseases in the *Back to Eden* book, a guide to herbal medicines and home remedies. Take turns reading the symptoms until we had the diseases down pat. "Hysteria" and "hydrophobia" (caused by wolf or rat bite) are best. We walk down the aisles, and every time we find a product with water, we gag, sob, convulse, act out the "dread of water" contortions symptomatic of wolf and rat bite. The store manager does this Amazon strut in high heels and shoulder pads—heaving and slinging her cannonball breasts. Head up, chin out. The store hardly seems large enough for her. When the phone rings, she squeals *Hello!* with game show expectancy. At some point, she'll grab me by the elbow, say, "I'll find you something to clean." All day long I ask people, mostly strangers, "Can I help you?" It's a small store. I know where everything is. Usually they want to feel better. For once, I feel kind of useful. I'll work for the health food store, at different locations, for more than ten years. It grounds me, pulls me through. Even when a customer is rude, or I'm fighting with a coworker, the store is something I can count on. I'm in the world, I have a task. Five days a week, sometimes six, I show up, I reach out to other people. It's a relief to belong somewhere.

In July 1984, when I'm six months sober, my coworkers Michelle and Pat buy me a coffee mug as a gift. Mike lived near this mall for awhile, in the woods. It was before I met him. He ate from the McDonald's Dumpster, timing it to get food when it was just thrown out. He had a friend who could catch fish from a river with his bare hands. He likes to talk about deer. His stories are like fables, myths he repeats. I don't know how much of a person's soul is visible in most people, what percentage is hidden in a back room, but Mike seems as though he is mostly soul. His body a gangly covering. When he listens to me, it's almost as if I'm in another world. Sometimes I try to pay better attention, the way he does, to everyone—the customers, their stories.

A big, friendly girl comes in the store once a week to buy carob stars. She's sort of shy, but always talks a lot. I weighed her a pound of stars, and she said, "There are so many accidents on 436. It's Blood Alley." Driving home from work, fire trucks were behind me because of an accident on Highway 50. Then, on 436, I get hit and pushed into another car. My car is totaled. It has no back to it anymore. My door won't open. My neck and leg hurt, but no one is hurt badly. There's a little boy in the car that hit me. A Navy guy was driving; he'd borrowed the car from a friend. But I never understood where the kid comes from. At most, he's eight years old. Worried I'd want his name. The kid keeps saying,

"I'm on parole." Parole? He's got on camouflage pants that match the driver's shirt, but it doesn't appear that he's either a friend or a relation. The boy's got long, messy, blond hair, and his eyes slant in. He sits next to me on the curb and smokes, says, "Once I made my mom nervous when I turned up the music on the radio. Caused a three-car accident." He takes a drag. I feel as though I should say something about the smoking. "My dad took the radio out of the car."

"You shouldn't smoke," I venture. The air is full of water; my hair is getting longer.

"I wave my cigarettes in front of my dad and dare him to stop me," the boy says. The cops are slow. "I don't have anything to do tonight," he says. He looks pleased to be in an accident. Keeps staring at me, saying, "You don't look scared at all." He says, "My mom was a wreck." Wherever I go, he trails after me. Our hearts beating in a weird orbit. It's almost 11 p.m., and this little kid keeps walking around the highway, smoking. He asks me, "Do you go to Winter Park High School?" He says, "I was going to drop out of school, but I've changed my mind." Can eight-year-olds drop out of school? When someone came to take me home, the boy said, "I'm sorry about everything." He stood there alone, said, "'Bye." Realized I never heard anyone ask the kid if he was okay.

It's as though I was hit by ghosts last night. That guy that hit me, the owner of the car, his insurance company—they all seem like weird ghostly voices. The guys lie about knowing each other. Someone gives me a cactus tree to save. I've already killed three plants. But I'm glad to be digging dirt out of the yard with my bare hands, trying to save this funny plant. When I cup the earth in my hands, I remember I'm a part of it, and the bruises, aches, dead car, ghost driver and company fade a little.

Catherine from Dry Dock shows up at Broadway. She cries when I tell her I got my six-month chip. She said, "I really like you, can't we be friends?" I really like her too, don't know why I veer away. I don't tell her that I want to find my son's grave. Pull up some grass. And do what with it? Hold it in my hand, stuff it in my purse, use my fingers to comb it into my hair. Chew the blades of grass and try to swallow? Push my fingernails down into the dirt where it's hard, pack it under my nails. And push further, dig and dig all night. Until I find what they put him in. Not wood I guess, what's that vinyl stuff—maybe that's inside the coffin. It's a very small coffin, baby coffin. Dig until I can fit, curled up, next to him. Then start pulling the soft handfuls back in. Over my feet, over my knees, like a damp blanket at the beach. Like when the wind comes up at the shore, and the sun goes down. You're mostly bare, so you pull the towel, wet from the sea, over your feet, up over your knees. It'll be like being buried in sand at the beach, but darker. Use my arms like shovels to scoop dirt, dark and heavy, to my neck, drifting down my chin. Then from my hair down. Cool over my forehead. Over my eyes, and the line between my eyes. I thought I heard Tommy cry. I could swear I heard him crying. Maybe he's not in this box. Maybe I should keep looking. I *could swear* I heard him—it was so sweet. Maybe if I said something of this to Catherine, said something true, I could come toward her.

When it's Tommy's birthday, I'm on the phone with Wendy from work. She knows. Her little boy starts singing. "What's he singing?" I asked. She was embarrassed, didn't wanted to tell me. She said, "It's just a coincidence." Then she said, "It's his favorite song. It's 'Happy Birthday.'" She's silent a minute, and I can hear the singing. Later she comes over to my apartment, my first nice one. White. Second floor. A fireplace. I go downstairs, sit on the steps to wait for them. Her son runs to me, sitting there. Puts his two toy trucks in my lap, laughing. It helps that these boys like me, Wendy's son, the boy in the accident. I'm glad they come toward me.

One night in 1989, I'm at work in the store, reading an article on relationships in the new *East West Journal*. It mentions a new book, *Women, Sex, and Addiction: A Search for Love and Power*, by Charlotte Davis Kaslo. I order a copy in hardcover. It says that shame is the root of addiction, that violence gives instant escape. "Most of these women don't really want to die, they want to kill the pain." The author said that to get well a person needed to give up suicide fantasies and threats "and make a commitment to live, for better or worse." A marriage to your own life.

I try it. Listening to her voice, I know, okay, close the door now. I can see it at the end of a hall, brown wood. Feel the ground under my feet. I shut the door. I turn around, face the other way. Into my life. I'm in my living room with this book in my hand, but I don't see it anymore. I see the hall and the door, and I hear her helping voice. Something shifts inside me, like a big rectangle of light, as if the rooms in my body shift into place. No longer threatened. As if my body understands that I'll stay.

Weeks later, the door looks tiny back there—I can see it without turning around. The more I walk, the lighter the hallway gets. It makes me think of sitting on the curb of Tangerine Avenue when I was eleven, knowing there would be a bright place up ahead when I grew up.

In 2009, three years after I've moved away from Orlando, I go back to the Broadway house for a meeting. It's nonsmoking now. Before I'd moved away to the beach in 2006, I'd driven into the parking lot here, thinking a meeting was about to start. But I wasn't going often enough, had the time wrong. Mike and Ray were there though, talking. So, I got to say good-bye. Ray said, "Stay in touch with us." But I hadn't.

A meeting is starting, lots of people arriving, parking between the trees, walking toward the door. I look for Mike. He's always easy to spot. So tall, and also, I could feel him in a crowd, or he sensed me. But he isn't outside. I'm about to go in, when I see that one of the men outside the front door is Ray. I hug him, Ray whom I've known since before I got sober, who said stay in touch. I'm so happy to see him. "Is Mike here?" I ask. Smiling. He's almost always there.

"I'm sorry," Ray said. It's registering on his face that he's going to be the one to tell me. "He died."

"What?"

"He died. Cancer." I've stepped out of myself, can see my face, open mouth. Staring at Ray. "I was with him," he says. "In the hospital."

"Why didn't you call me?"

"No one had your phone number," Ray said. He'd said stay in touch. He's not blaming me.

I have one photo of Mike, with a shark that he caught at the pier. He's beaming. He's so proud, loves this photo. So he gives it to me. Once, he disappeared, after he married, and his wife died, after he gave the insurance money away to anyone who asked, and he was broke, and went away and drank. I was in school then, away. When Mike came back to Orlando, he told me, "It's hard getting sober when you're older." He was in a halfway house. It was 1996. I was teaching three classes, managing a bookstore, and running a literary organization as a volunteer. When I came home from my jobs, I was tired. And he'd call me nightly, talk for hours. I wanted to shower, eat, relax. I stopped answering the phone automatically.

Mike got sober, all over again. He was sober for the rest of his life. In the early days, we had the same sobriety date, except his was a year before mine. To celebrate, the recovery group had a cake for both of us, and I remember candles, which can't be right—why would there be candles? But there was something bright. The room was packed, and everyone stood around Mike and me, wishing us well. It doesn't seem as though he can be ashes in an urn at Ray's house. I can still see him. When I tell Mary this, my sponsor from Orlando, she says, "Mike isn't ashes." I'm ashamed that I've believed this, worried that I've gone so far away from Mike. Forgetting that he is unburnable, unburned, unburnt.

When I meet Ray at the pier at eight in the morning, he says, "You're the only person I asked to come." It's so kind, giving me a chance to say good-bye. Ray and I haven't spent much time in each other's company for more than a decade. I don't know if we've ever spoken on the phone before. But he'd called me at home after I'd seen him at the meeting and learned that Mike died. Ray had said we could meet on Saturday or Sunday. Whichever day is better for me. I know he's nervous; he calls me "Ma'am." He's known me twenty-seven years. He's never called me anything but Kelle.

There are a few silent men standing in corners of the pier, the ocean out front. Ray has a backpack, opens it. He'd been keeping Mike's ashes in his house all this time. He opens a plastic bag. I thought that when a body burned, the ashes would be black like a house or a tree, but his are the color of sand. Six pounds, the weight of a baby. The sun's getting higher. Ray says that he and Mike would sit here all day fishing, even in rain, even at night. They hated to leave. I know what he means, what it's like to turn away from the ocean. When Ray reaches into the bag, it feels as if he's reaching inside our friend's body, everything slippery—heart, lungs. He's got a small handful of ash. If I could, I'd reach in to touch the bones in his face, but it's too much. I back away from Ray.

When Mike was in the hospital, dying, Ray said the room was always full of people visiting. Mike had known he had cancer, but hadn't told anyone, took no treatment. When he'd collapsed at home, Ray was the one who went to him, drove him to the hospital. Stayed with him. When Ray scatters the handful on the other side of the pier, I follow from a distance. Ash blows around his legs. Mike kissed my forehead one night. We'd gone somewhere in my car, and he'd opened the passenger door to leave, turned back. When he kisses me, I can feel he loves me, that he thinks I'm worthy, good. I try to see who he sees.

I keep having to shade my eyes. Ray's T-shirt is soaked. He walks back to the bench, the open backpack, takes out the whole bag. When he pours it all out over the edge of the pier, five-hundred feet down, Mike's bones lift up. Phosphorescent. Like the rings around a planet. What is the prayer? Should I be saying a prayer? Maybe Ray and I together make one. The surfers, the corner men, we all watch the glow above the water. It sinks like a river in the ocean. 'Bye, sweetheart, I say inside my auditorium. "Mary said that's not him," I tell Ray. Ray says, "Mike always wore this world lightly." He looks out over the ocean, the horizon. "I like how it opens out," Ray says. It's hard to turn away. He hugs me good-bye so many times it's as though we're never leaving.

Mirror

In Florida, especially in August, rain falls like a bucket dumped; it falls out of a sunny sky. You can walk in and out of rain. Humidity a sheen on skin, hair. The watery air smothering, so real rain is a relief. The way it announces itself in the dirt first, dim earth, and then the air smells like stones. The stones love rain too, wake up from their sleep. It's 1986. At work, I'm back at the busy Winter Park store. I guess the owner thinks I can take it. I'm twenty-four. On my lunch breaks I need a break from the constant talking, the customers and their health problems. Everyone talking about their bodies. People ask me to read their eyes, their faces. Help them do a fast or lose weight or stop sneezing. Sleep, lots of people weren't sleeping. The people with serious diseases scared me—cancer, MS. I had books, indices, but no medical training. "What should I eat?" they asked. One woman just talks about her elusive doctor boyfriend, the gifts she buys him. And her colon. She finds me hiding down one of the aisles, straightening the rows of bottles. People were always giving up coffee, as if it were stealing or arson. "It drains your adrenal glands," said a woman who never seemed to age. Customers would confess to eating sugar, dairy. I'd say, "It's okay." All the listening makes me dizzy—I forget to breathe. They range up and down the vitamin aisle, asking, "What's good for me?" Sometimes I'd sit in the circle of stones in front of the store, stare at the yellow flowers, their hallelujah.

The health food store is separate from the rest of the shopping center. It's along a perpendicular strip. I have to cross the wide parking lot to go inside the mall. Get away completely. I'd stopped going to Broadway so much for meetings, because some people had started to say, "Hope you'll open up tonight." "We know you have some interesting things to say." I found a new meeting in a little green house just down the street from the Winter Park store. They don't care if I talk or not. It's a relief to just sit there and listen.

Two years sober, I got my own apartment. The nice one. Lived alone. The quiet helped, the door that I could shut and lock. I'd moved in with my counselor first, the women who'd run the Navy alcohol treatment program. She'd turned her home into a kind of halfway house for recovering women. She lived there, her teenage daughter, me, and two other women. The first time I went over her house, it was for dinner. Lasagna with meat. I was so nervous, I didn't tell her I was vegetarian. Just ate it. Once I was out of my parents' house, in the care of another, my relationship with my parents began to improve. I think they started to trust that I would live. And not living with them eased their attempts to control me. They didn't see me as an adult, but I stopped being a child and began a kind of perpetual late adolescence.

At work, on my lunch break, I often walked across the tar toward the quiet of the mall. Something heavy fell off of me, like a tire off a car. I didn't know it was there until I felt the lightness afterward. Nights, in the room at the green house, I could close my eyes while I held someone's hand, and I'd see my hand in a room of light. Even though I'd been sober more than two years, I kept forgetting that this was my extra life. That I'd died in 1983, so in this life, I could do anything. Sometimes in traffic, the light would remind me. Not the traffic lights or sun. I'd have my hands on the wheel, and it would feel like my car didn't have a roof, as if it was a convertible, and light would fall on me, in columns like rain, or a hand touching me. Well-being. Peace. Normally, I shook a lot, a kind of low-level vibrating, a nervous humming. I weighed so little, coworkers, customers thought I was anorexic. Approached me with questions as if they were intervening. "I wanted to feed you hamburgers," one customer said. I ate, but sometimes felt so terrorized, the food would hurt. I couldn't calm down. Meetings helped and the light in the car. When heavy things started falling off of me, I didn't know I'd been carrying them. Didn't know what they were.

All my boyfriends come from the Winter Park store, one after the other. It was easy for them to talk to me—I'm in the store every day. Cheerful, bagging their groceries. So familiar, they think they know me. One of the Winter Park ex-boyfriends, a beautiful man, is in line to be rung up. I'm at the other register, my back to him. He says, "There are freckles on Kelle's back—it must be summer." He says it as though he misses me. "I'm going to France for the summer," he says. An architect, he's going to build something. By that time, I've lost my apartment and am living with strangers I've found in the newspaper, in a three-bedroom house. But I want to live alone. I know I'm being manipulative, that I'm a bad tenant, a risk, but I say, "I could house-sit for you. I could take care of your cat."

"Okay," he says. I'm shocked he's agreed. I'm a terrible housekeeper. But he hasn't really known me that long. He's never lived with me. We'd broken up because I fell in love with another customer at the store, a man who made stained glass. When we were going out, the architect had said, "I want to make a commitment to you." It had felt so planned, as if our relationship was a house he was building. When he asked what I felt, I kept reaching into an empty room. He was beautiful. But meticulous, cautious. I wanted to mess things up. Once when we were together, he'd forgotten to take out the trash. We were already in bed, falling asleep. "I'll do it," I said. Throwing off the sheet. I walked down the stairs, to the deck, dragged the trash can through the grass, under the trees, to the curb. I could see him at the window, watching me naked on the street.

His place is a tree house, three stories up, but only wide enough for one person to live here. He designed it. I'm supposed to pay the utilities and a modest rent. The upstairs I call the Cathedral of Trees because the ceiling is churchy, the walls all windows surrounded by trees. Under the kitchen counter, I come across his will—nothing for me—just my name listed under "People to Notify." Find $236.13 in coins in a giant Tupperware. I borrow it until the ex-boyfriend comes home. Roll them out and get groceries for a few weeks. It's fine at first, but when I get down to the dime rolls, the cashiers started rolling their eyes. They won't take the pennies. The ex-boyfriend doesn't like the Van Morrison song I put on his answering machine. "It's getting louder every time I call," he said. His cat sleeps on my chest. I accidently spill purple grape juice on his couch cushion. The toaster catches fire, and two firemen come by.

But mostly it's quiet. It's the first time I've been solitary in a long time. My grandfather had died that year. I have his rocking chair at the architect's house. Laura from work helps me haul it in. Sometimes I miss my grandfather so badly, I can't stop crying. There's no one there to stop me. It goes on for hours. I need to touch something my grandfather has touched, sit on the floor with my face in his chair, arms around the arms. Brown upholstery scratchy on my face.

My grandfather came to me in a dream right after he'd died. Still in the hospital—we stood on the stairs together. He was desolate—but not for me. He was calling for Nana. But I showed up, wearing her apron with all the fruit, orange slices, cherries, lemons on the cloth. I was all he had. He was so tall, he had to lean far down to put his head on my shoulder, crying for her. I told Nana. I said, *he's looking for you.*

I hold onto his rocking chair, rock it until it's a boat. When I get up from the chair, to wash my face, I forgot myself, as if my body is a coastline. Forgot to forget my soul. I go into the bathroom with the wall of glass, stand there for a long time, and see someone else in the mirror.

Later, I see paintings of it—neophytes looking for their souls. In each painting, a Japanese girl wraps herself in a piece of silk. Sometimes only a band, like a tie around her waist. And the girl leans, her body swirling like a fish or a wave, into a hand mirror, looking for her soul. But I didn't know how to look, the day I see the woman in the right side of the mirror. Not held there, but the glass is the place I can see her.

She looks exactly like the me I'd wanted to be—eyes, mouth. But beautiful, the fear gone. She said, "I've been with you always. Long before now. I'll be here long after." She is a companion in the way that you are a companion to yourself. "I'll always stay," she said. I don't know how she talks to me—words more than voice. But she's my soul. I'm not alone. Ever.

When the architect comes home, angry at the state of things, he says I have to leave. A girl at the Orlando store said I can move in with her old roommate, a painter. A two-bedroom apartment. At night, the new roommate cooks something in his bedroom next door to mine. It smells purple. Sometimes he screams as if he's being tortured. In the morning, there's no explanation. He stands next to me in the small kitchen, pouring orange juice in a glass. Sometimes his son stays over, in the room with the screaming. When his mother shows up, I want to say, "Listen, there's something wrong. The air smells purple. I don't know if it's safe." I don't know why the girl from work never mentioned anything strange.

My roommate gets a job painting at one of the topless bars, Circus Circus or the Booby Trap. I think he's painting scenery—it's unclear. Guys from the bar start showing up at the apartment. One makes my roommate give him a key. I find a new place to live on the road to school. I'm still working on my B.A. in English at UCF in Orlando. The apartment is cheap. No closet. But there's a pool. When I tell my roommate that I'm leaving, the guy from the bar shows up at our place with a girl named Kelly. "She's going to sleep in your room," my roommate said. Replacing me with someone else with my name. She's a dancer from out of town; she's going to work at the bar. In the days before I leave, I go into the bathroom across the hall, the one I share with my roommate. I can't remember if I look for the woman in the mirror, or if she just appears. I know I have to be willing to see her. She's there in the glass.

I see her more than once there, for briefer amounts of time than the first time. But now, her face is my face. As though she's always here, if I'm not afraid to look. When I see her, I know that no one is ever lost. Tommy isn't lost. Neither is my grandfather. For the first time, I'm grateful for being alive, as an everyday thing. Not just in flashes. I thought I had to become someone I would be willing to approve of, love. I didn't know I was her already.

I see her one more time, when a coworker leaves the state and lets me rent her condo on a lake. Quiet. It's funny, these were the condos where Bill used to live—right across the parking lot is his old door. The bathroom has a big glass mirror. I tape poems around all the edges, but there's a clear space. When I see the woman in the mirror, I almost tip over. A small window behind me. Two floors up. When I see her, I can't remember what year it is. Basics, I can't remember basics. Where I live. The floor slants. I look outside at a street sign to get my balance. I look away.

Palindrome

1.

I'm living alone in the cheap, closetless apartment on Alafaya Trail. Sometimes after work, I get a six-pack of nonalcoholic beer. I know I shouldn't drink something that tastes like alcohol. That "nonalcoholic" doesn't mean no alcohol, just a very low percentage. I know people in meetings who've gotten drunk on cold medicine, mouthwash. It's dangerous for me. In these early days, there's still something self-destructive that won't let go completely. Soon I'll run into one of my brother's old girlfriends in a meeting, and she'll ask me if it's okay for her to drink nonalcoholic wine, to bring it to a party. It gives me pause. I'm so used to only considering myself. I say yes, I think it's okay. Though it nags me even as I'm telling her this, as if there is a part of me that would take back every word. When I don't see her at that meeting again, or any other, the regret I feel is sickening. She'd been brand new, someone who trusted me to be truthful.

That night after work, I skip my meeting, sit on the barstool in the kitchen drinking a couple bottles down fast. Read lines from Merwin's poems taped to the refrigerator. I'd found a photo of Merwin in a book from 1968. He's young, in a flannel shirt, leaning on an old truck. One of his fingers is balanced on the other, making a circle that rests on the engine grate. It's sunny, but it must be cold; his sleeves are buttoned to the wrist, trees bent in the wind. Like a farmer, I'd thought, standing in the bright grass with leaves blowing behind him, seeming to fill the bed of his pickup. I find lines from Merwin in Denis Johnson's *The Stars at Noon* and retype them on my typewriter, tape them up. I'd never been to the poet's island, though my mother had. I lived on a smaller one as a child, and when my mother came back from the volcano, so happy, with a straw bag clasped with gold and a white muumuu, I knew it was a place I'd never go, like the island of flowers.

In the big, gold chair I took from my parents' house, I read Merwin's poems, instead of just the lines taped around the house like instructions. It's the chair I sat in when I held my son for a few minutes, before my relatives took him away. The last time I saw him. He was four days old. Sometimes my next-door neighbor beats his girlfriend. When I come home from the store, up the stairs, I often have to pass his corridor of friends leaning on the rail, spilling out his front door. My neighbor has a deep scar under his eye. He usually tries to bar my way, inviting me in. I always refuse, so they don't like me. When I swim in the pool, they yell obscenities my way. In my apartment, I can hear the girlfriend screaming, *Hit me again. Go ahead.* And he does, even though his friends are still there. Her head bangs on the wall behind me.

Her hair is blond, long. Bloated face, pretty eyes. Voice like a scratch. She always looks either ready to bolt or half-asleep. Going to work one morning, I find a pale condom, a knife, and somebody's khakis on the concrete outside my door. The neighbor guy starts showing up at my work. "I want to learn about vitamins," he says. He gets me explaining why I don't drink. "I want to stop drinking," he says. "Maybe you can help me." I mainly straighten the shelves when he visits, keeping my eyes on the bottles. He and his girlfriend get an eviction notice on their door. Maybe he thought he could move in with me. Bang my head on the wall.

Briefly, I have a new boyfriend whom I meet in the store. He buys me Merwin's new book. At night I pull my gold chair directly in front of the fan and read. I recite his poem "Come Back" to everyone I know.

2.

Before I'd moved out of the architect's house, I took a job meant for him. His beauty had attracted an agency that left a message inviting him to be an extra in a TV commercial at Pleasure Island. In his absence, I accepted, inviting my friend Billy from the store. I was told to dress up as if it were New Year's Eve, told I'd been dancing in the street.

In *An Angel at My Table*, Janet Frame said, "I had little experience of many people; I knew them only in my heart." At twenty-two, she'd sewn an everglaze dress for her first dance at Town Hall, recognizing the Maxima, Military Two-Step, the Destiny from dances in the hospital, thinking, "Ask me, ask me," and no one did. A customer in the health food store said I should rent the movie of her life, that Janet Frame reminded him of me. I was embarrassed to see myself so clearly on screen, someone scoured open, always in need of a dark coat, a disguise to manage shopping, errands in the world, and I came to dislike the customer for noticing. I was just a clerk, but everyone wanted attention—these customers, the beautiful architect speaking from a room far within.

Sober, I didn't think my dancing skills were good enough for television, so I enrolled in a dance school, saying I didn't need eight weeks of lessons, just a quick course for my acting career. My teacher like a middle-aged waiter holding my arms like plates.

We were in a mirrored room with barres as for ballet. Alcohol on his breath in the afternoon. He guided my feet through the maze of shoes marked on the floor, like the chalk-drawn feet of crime victims, though I was pretty sure that these waltzlike boozy steps weren't practical tools for my commercial.

Billy picked me up in a suit—it was cold, but I didn't wear a coat, just a black bustier, tiny flounced skirt, shoulders freezing, dancing outside all night to the same minute or two of "Love Shack," my dance teacher not having taught me any moves to the B-52s, but by then I didn't care, flailing around when the music started.

The only business open was a candy shop. Full of chocolate and coffee, trying to stay warm, awake, getting paid our seventy dollars only if we stayed until morning, the full twelve hours. Before dawn we were herded into a theater, fed boxed lunches, then maybe thirty of us found an unlocked door, a game room, and slept on the floor, head to foot, for warmth, the TV people finding us like the police, making us dance until it felt like a drug, the lamps at night indistinguishable from my own closed eyes, my body at rest with everyone in the arcade.

3.

I kept dropping out of school. Wouldn't do the assignments, wouldn't show up. When I was close to meeting the requirements for my bachelor's degree, I just stopped going completely. Got 3 F's. Grade point destroyed, figured I'd never go back. But the teacher from my first creative writing class, the one who had showed me the boy's story, he'd visit me at the health food store. When I'd been twenty and drinking every day, late for classes, absent for weeks, he had been my only friend at school. I'd sit on the couch in his office with the naked female mannequin and wall-sized collage of models from magazines, and be calmed. He was fond of me like a troubled character in a novel, pulling for me. In the health food store, the owner would say, "You may be book smart, but you sure are stupid." For years my teacher comes in, buys vitamins, says, "Come back to school." So, I do.

In 1989, right before I graduate, another teacher tells me I've won a departmental award, for outstanding undergraduate poet. He's smiling. I ask, "Are you sure?" There's a ceremony. For the first time, I stand up in front of people and read a few poems. I have to rest my hands on the podium because they're trembling. My voice shakes. But it doesn't seem to matter—everyone quiet, listening.

I decide to go to graduate school even though, with work, I can take only a couple of classes at time. UCF accepts me into its new program in creative writing. A woman, Pamela, from one of my undergraduate writing classes, stops in at the health food store. She's always in a rush, blond hair flying, fast talking. I know she works for UCF's tutoring center and admire her for this, her good job. Once I'd worn a nicer dress to work at the store, and my coworker Lana said, "You could be a secretary in that." I'd been a kind of secretary for the Weapons Department in Spain, but hadn't applied for that job, just checked a box. Neither Lana nor I knew how to find work as a secretary, how to get a sit-down job. At the UCF tutoring center, there's a woman whose job is parallel in responsibility to Pamela's. "She hired an assistant," Pamela says, scanning the vitamin shelves. "I don't have an assistant." It's 1990. I know a door is opening. But I have to try, I have to speak. "I'd love to tutor," I say. It happens so fast. "Well, if Kathy can hire someone, so can I," Pamela says.

After that, I work at the health food store only on the weekends. At the center, I provide tutoring in writing to Pamela's ESOL students. It's more money, $6 an hour, and everyone in the office is kind. It's an atmosphere of helpfulness. I love working with one person at a time, the pace of it. It's such a relief to have a skill, to know what to do. No one here says I'm stupid. Before workshop one night, Don, my poetry teacher who told me about my first writing award, is smiling at me. He says that the poem I submitted to the department's literary magazine has won first place. There's publication and a check for $100.

When I'm working on my master's degree, my first writing teacher rents me the apartment on the back of his house in Oviedo. Close to Orlando, but rural. Originally, orange groves and celery farms. Now it's just quiet. Up three flights of rickety stairs. For hours every day, my teacher's dalmation, Pal (Palindrome), clangs her chain up and down my stairs, like Igor, some damned thing. At the landing, she peers into my window screen, a shadow dog, clanks back down.

The house is a hundred-year-old mansion he'd bought with his book money. On Lake Charm. Surrounded by huge old oaks, Spanish moss hanging like hair. I like old houses, but his spooks me—like being inside a game of Clue, the rooms always unfamiliar, angular, humid, the house too large to air-condition. He loans me a copy of *Breakfast at Tiffany's* with black mold on the pages.

My teacher tells me he's going away for a couple days. I'm not allowed in the house while he's gone. But a door from my apartment leads to a stairwell and the kitchen below. "I keep it unlocked" he said. "In case of fire." He's long divorced from a tiny, blond ballerina. Years ago, he was having a secret affair with a student in my class, another tiny, blond ballerina.

I didn't like being shut out of the house. My friend Laurel had never been inside, so I invite her. She comes over and brings her camera. In one photo, I wear an antique-y sleeveless dress and bone fishnets, pose shoeless on the porch hammock—one foot in the air. For another shot, I lean over the widow's walk to wave at Laurel on the front lawn. Far inside the house, we find a tiny room off the kitchen, a stuck doorknob, so I lean into it. When the door opens, something crystal or glass crashes to the floor. It's odd, as if it has been placed to fall if the door is opened. There may have been a key in the door. Shutting it, I see a murky window that looks out onto the yard.

There have been other student affairs by then too, a blond undergrad who interviews him for the paper, saying she wants to capture his flavor. He takes her to a dark country bar on Highway 50. For a long time he sees a young woman who looks like a twelve-year-old boy. I don't find him attractive myself. After my teacher returns, he stands in the yard, holding an opened package. I come downstairs, hoping to get into my car, but he calls me over. He said there is a little room off the kitchen, a room where he does some writing—he keeps an old typewriter in there—and some object in the room is now broken. I smiled patiently, too nervous to hear exactly what I've broken. He speaks very, very slowly. A game to make me confess, and the game makes me angry.

He stares at me silently, pausing several times to do this. Then he takes a book out of the package in his hand, says it has arrived with no return address. It was Ann Bernays's *Professor Romeo*. He asks, "Why would someone send this?" Did I have any idea? I think the book is brilliant, necessary. His perplexed face—how could he be surprised? It reminds me of my own pretending.

Don, my poetry teacher, recommends me for a writing retreat at an artists' residency center about an hour away, near the beach. It's free. I'm going to live with writers, composers, and painters from all over the country for three weeks. I get the time off from work. Before I leave for the retreat, Don tells me the English Department selected me for their outstanding graduate student award. There's a ceremony again, a reading. It's 1993. At the podium, I remembered trembling there in 1989, how fast I'd read. I'm still a little nervous, but not overwhelmed. It's as if the poems carry me when I read them.

The artists' center is secluded in the woods. A sign reads, "Artists at Work." No one has ever called my writing work. It's as though the place itself respects me. In the painting studio, a beautiful barnlike space of cedar and glass looking out on the dark woods, a composer takes my hand, twirls me. I didn't know I could be this happy.

When I come home, I'm so lonely, I go to an open mike at a coffee house. The owner befriends me, says, "I'm thinking of starting a different kind of open mike." He doesn't say what kind. "Would you run it for me?" I don't know how to run anything, but I feel as if I should just say yes. Figure it out later. "Yes." It becomes a literary organization that I create and run for five years, with a reading series, writing workshops, annual contests. It made me feel as though I can make something happen.

By the time I finish grad school, I've moved away from Lake Charm, and my teacher has brain cancer, seizures, trouble teaching. A red-haired girl loved him. The department chair asked if I would take over his classes for the semester, if necessary. It was my teacher who had marched me into the chair's office two years prior and announced, "Kelle is available to teach," as if it were the most lucky news. While I'd been at the tutoring center, I'd started teaching test prep classes, and then a private international language school opened up next door. Pamela got hired to teach full-time, brought me in too (though in 1994, when a new director arrived and required all staff to have an MA in linguistics, I was out of a job). I'd walked across campus to my teacher's office, and he'd helped me. Without my even asking. The next semester, I was an adjunct instructor of English for UCF and for two community colleges, teaching seven classes at four different campuses.

To the department chair, I said, "Yes, I can take over his classes." A guilt close to my guilt over the dalmation. One day, I'd seen another dog with Pal in the yard. She'd been old then, elderly even—I should have chased off the male dog but was unsure what to do, how to interrupt behind glass. Pal had puppies in the garage, and that year she died. When the puppies were just born, suckling, exhausting her, hills of vanilla-colored blankets surrounding them, my teacher asked over and over, "How could this happen?" His questions always soft, as if he were only talking to himself, overheard.

The Shoe Museum

The city of Brockton died years before I was born, but people kept on living there, one big cemetery. Empty shoe factories like massive headstones with thousands of tiny windows punched out, as if those inside had tried to flee. My dad was born in Brockton, like me. They had no car, not ever. No car, no TV, and sometimes only candles, no electricity. Once, when he was a boy, my dad was in the bathroom, on the seat, with a candle in his hand. He wondered what the candle in his hand could do, touched it to the curtains at the window, and watched everything go up. He won't tell me much about Brockton, growing up. "You'll just put it in a poem," he says, sulking. As if I'm nothing but a spy who took over his daughter's body. An eavesdropper. But I know some facts.

It was a town of mostly farms, until Micah Faxon invented Brockton's retail shoe sales. There was no right or left shoe then, just a shoe you shaped into comfortability by wear. Micah cut the leather in town and traveled with his shoes on horseback to Boston. This was before sizes and molds and lasts—you just tried on a shoe to see if it fit. Micah like a prince with a glass slipper coming to find you.

The shoe factories were born when a sewing machine was invented that made it possible to sew the top of the shoe to the bottom, instead of nailing them together. By the beginning of the twentieth century, the corner of Belmont and Main, near where Nana Smith, my dad's mother, will be born, live, and die, the sun is bright on the street, crisscrossed with telephone wires, an iron quilt above the city. Black carriages of cars like funeral veils line up before the grist wheel, arched roofs raised in prayer. The street hums with electricity, the first power station in the country. Even Edison comes to town to see the first electric street railway.

My aunt Julia, Tommy's mother, worked in one of the shoe factories. It was her first job out of high school. Now the factories are closed, and the work is gone. But there's a new train to Boston, thirty minutes to South Station. One of the old shoe factories has been turned into expensive lofts. The place is called SoCo, for "So Cool" and "So Convenient," and directionally, south of Court Street. You can get a ceiling of pure light, tall glass atriums good for sewing bone buttons, tiny stitches. A place of concentration, open sky.

Since 1999, I've been thinking about shoes. In 1996, a book had come out about the children in Woburn who died from leukemia, their water contaminated. A few years later, out of the blue, Sue Anne from work said she used to live near Brockton, that her husband's company had tested the land in Brockton for a bus station, but it had been too contaminated to build on. Then, Sue said she'd seen an article from *Boston Magazine* with high childhood leukemia deaths in Brockton. I looked the article up online. I thought it said 100 deaths. What was the time frame? How many children have died since Tommy died? A few months later, I was invited to a money seminar. Broke, I went and was introduced to a woman who told me that she had self-published a book about her son who had died from leukemia after growing up in Brockton. She said that she felt his death was environmentally related. I always felt there was something wrong with the city. It felt so gray—the sky, the trees like stick figures reaching out in panic.

In 2006, in Boston, the Commonwealth filed a complaint against Brockton for pollutants in the public water, fined the poor city. There's now going to be an $86-million sewage-treatment upgrade. But I'm not thinking phosphorus, chlorine, fecal coliform, ammonia—I'm thinking carcinogens, lethal environmental hazards. I'm thinking of the leukemia that came from the ground in Woburn, from tanneries, the making of shoe leather. All the Woburn kids who died from leukemia.

Summers, I'd ask to see my son. He was so close. On the Cape, staying with my mother's parents in the Yarmouth Campground, a circle cut in the woods, train track running in a field behind the house, across the entrance to the campground. "Can we go to Brockton today," I'd ask my dad, "to Tommy's cemetery?" I wouldn't say *grave*. Whispering in the front yard, the attic of the house behind us, its one dark window listening. A secret. When I'd wanted to go to Tommy's funeral, my father had said, "No one knows where he came from." He'd said, "I'm not saying you can't go, but you have to call his parents, and ask them if you can be there." My relatives. Tommy's adoptive parents. I couldn't ask. I didn't go. I'm a secret too, a secret mother.

Our family was inside the house, and to the left at the picnic table, a round barbecue. "Everyone will ask where we're going," my dad said. As if that was a solid reason not to go to Brockton. "And I don't know if I can even find it. I'd have to ask . . ." Whom would he ask? His relatives, the ones we can't hurt, and if we ask for directions, we'll hurt them. We'll remind them that I gave them Tommy, and Tommy died. My dad is looking around at the ground, as though he's dropped several things at once. And that's that. We can't separate from the others, we can't tell them where we're going, we can't ask directions, we can't hurt the relatives. It's an hour drive to Brockton. I imagine it is all uphill, the highway climbing after I cross the bridge, past the cranberry bogs, and the white boulder walls, the pine trees like individual steeples. When I leave the Cape, the houses look sad until I get to Boston. The in-between. Brockton is in the in-between.

I've had plans to get there myself. Once, I left my family at Nana and Gramp's house in the campground, and took the Plymouth-Brockton bus to Boston, to see Frank who'd worked with me at the health food store in Florida. I slept with his two cats on the floor. My bus home left after dark. I didn't want to leave the city, so took the latest returning bus. It was the Fourth of July, and all around me people went in and out of stores, until it was dark. Then they surrounded me in one big parade. I liked their voices, how they reminded me of the first voices I heard. I kept my suitcase in a locker at the station until I boarded. Around ten, my bus had been near Brockton, and it was going to stop. I thought of getting off the bus with the handful of dollars I had left. I could call my relatives and say, "I've come to visit." Or, I could stay in the train station all night, and call in the morning, ask them for directions to the cemetery. Or, I could get off the bus and just walk, let my feet feel the ground, and ask strangers to point me the right way. I could sleep on the grass beside Tommy, all night. No one would see me there. It's dark. I'd find a pay phone, call my parents, lie. Say I'm staying one more night in Boston.

I didn't even stand up. Or reach for my bag. The bus just carried me over the bridge. Cargo. Once, as a way to access my subconscious to find out what I wanted, I wrote with my left—nondominant—hand. I used a crayon. I had to buy a box of crayons to do this. When I wrote the first question with my left hand, it was wobbly, like a child's, as if I were just learning cursive. The question read: "Why don't you go to him?" I wrote back with my right hand, said that I wanted my new boyfriend to go with me. He seemed practical, more practical than me. But when I'd asked him, he'd looked at me sorrowfully, as if I were an animal, one of his cats, in pain. He had a very sorrowful face. He'd nod and listen and appear convinced, looking as if he'd love me forever. He'd go across the street to school and sit in my friend's office and tell her how much he loved me. But he wouldn't lift a finger. Wouldn't go. I wrote with my left hand again. The second question read: "You have a car. You have a vacation. Why don't you go?" I had a car I'd bought for $500, an orange Oldsmobile. People drove old cars across the country all the time. They unfolded maps. I would get lost, no doubt. I was nervous about reading a map, trusting the blue and red rivers to get me where I wanted to go. And once there, I'd have to ask, "Where is he? Where is my son?" Asking quietly because no one could know I was asking. It felt almost shameful, my wanting to find him when it seemed as though I had no right, or little right. As if I'd just been the vehicle, the receptacle. Not the real mother. Not the responsible people who flew across the country to take him, to take care of him every day, a married couple, into their own home. A family.

Over the years, my asking my parents became a blur. But in 1998, I was in a car with my father's mother, Nana Smith, who had lived in Brockton all her life. She was giving us directions to Calvary. Being driven by others is a form of captivity—it's hard to know the way when I'm not driving.

The stones spell the cemetery name across the grass. It's so big, you could see it from the sky, from a low plane, like HELP written in the sand or snow. Help. Nana Smith helps me with the flowers. The florist is nearby, and inside there is a patio of flowers. She said Tommy liked pink carnations. "He liked the petals," she said. So, I got those, and a yellow rose. My mom brought a spade and water in a plastic watering can.

My dad helped me dig, but once the flowers were in the ground, the rose on the stone ledge, they agreed all at once to leave me alone, and walked off as if they had somewhere to go. I buried my silver fish ring with the turquoise eyes in the dirt. It was the closest thing I had to a toy. I can't tell you when it happened, when I heard his voice. I know I was alone. I tried to hide my head behind the stone, so my family couldn't see me, so I could be unseen with my son. I didn't want to be careful, to keep myself calm—I wanted to pay attention to him, not keep my face emotionless for others.

I'd only heard his voice when he was born, when he cried. And little breaths, tiny contented sounds when I held him. His crying when I gave him away. And once, on the phone with Julia who'd been calling for my dad, I'd heard Tommy in the background— "la, la, la," he'd said. He was singing. He was only fourteen months old when he died. He wasn't speaking in sentences. How old is a soul? And how do the dead talk anyway? How do you hear the dead talk? I have no idea. But when I sat there alone on the grass in front of his stone, he said, "You're here!" with more joy than I have ever heard in my life. I'd been afraid he'd be mad at me for taking so long to get there. For not knowing how to save enough money to fly there myself, to rent a car, to be brave enough to ask directions to the cemetery, to find it alone. To visit him. But he wasn't mad at all. I heard it in his voice, his gladness. He loved me. I was his mother. I've never heard the dead before or since. The force field lifting just long enough for me to hear his voice.

Each year after that, I went to Calvary with my family—once Nana Smith's half sister came, once my nephew came and helped me dig to plant yellow tulips. I tried to pick the most fun-looking flowers, the happiest. The last time Nana Smith went with me, she had Alzheimer's. She'd been Tommy's caretaker when my relatives worked. I wanted to ask her to tell me about him, but I couldn't. And now she was forgetting. That trip, in the backseat of the car with Nana Smith, the return trip, was the only time I cried in front of anyone in my family. Except for the day my dad told me Tommy died—but that was an uncontrollable blur of grief. This time my grief is stark. It was terrible. I felt so unprotected. My mom turned her head a little from the passenger seat. To the left. Tense. The front seat was tense. In a way, they are like children I am trying to trick. I'm trying to trick them into thinking I'm okay. Nana Smith covers my hand with her hand on the vinyl seat. It's summer, my palm is hot, the vinyl is sticky, ridged. It feels as if she has a dozen rings on her fingers, pressing into mine, hard. But her hand is almost bare of jewelry, skin cool, her grip increasing in strength, as if she's relieved to finally see what I need, and to know what to do. She comforts me.

In the summer of 2003, I rented a car, and met Nana Smith's half sister, Anne. Nana Smith was in an assisted living facility by then, briefly, before she would run away. Before she'd be put in a hospital where she refused to eat, where she died. I had called Anne and asked her if I could see Nana Smith. She said, "Yes, I'll help you see your grandmother." But when I'd arrived, Nana said, "I don't know what to say to you without your parents here." She was scared of me. I'd been late, which had been an upset. The worry had made Nana ill. She wasn't herself. Afterward, I asked Anne how to get to Calvary, and she said, "I'll show you." I followed her car in my rental car. At the stoplights, I wrote down streets, turns, anything direction-wise to help me later. I had a little journal that I balanced on the steering wheel.

It's 2006. I have an appointment at the Brockton Shoe Museum. I want to look around. But first I'm going with my parents to visit my son's grave. They live in Massachusetts now, for half the year. I'm visiting. My father is aggravated about going to Brockton this summer. His mother, Nana Smith, has died just weeks before. I was coming to see her, I had a ticket. But she died. I missed her. I missed her funeral. I signed a guest book that the funeral home set up online. Relatives I don't know signed it. One typed in a Millay poem, with a woman who disappears down a dark path.

I didn't know anyone in my family liked poetry. These unknown relatives use nicknames I don't know. Maybe my dad is just upset. I should let him be upset. His mom died.

The florist beside Calvary has had a fire. It's ashy. My parents are driving. They're flummoxed by the fire. I need to buy flowers. "There's a Walmart back the way we came," I say. "It's too far," my mom says, irritated. We still don't know the way here very well, without a guide, without Nana Smith. It's slow going. We look for flowers in the immediate vicinity to avoid getting lost. My dad and I walk into a derelict store in a derelict shopping plaza, with clothes on tables on the sidewalk. Mom waits in the car. There is a nice, dark-haired cashier in the beat-up store selling home supplies. Men are holding beams of wood, standing in line at the cash register. The cashier's skin is like bluish milk, as if he never goes to the beach, his eyes red-rimmed, and when I ask, "Do you know where I can buy flowers?" he says, "That's a good question." It feels almost like a compliment. I would like to take him for coffee, and maybe date him, but I don't live here. And if we lived together, we would be so poor (this place can't pay much at all), even our electricity would be wan. We'd sit across the table from each other in the weak light wondering how to leave. But I feel as though I belong in this dark place, that I should house-hunt here.

As we drive away, my mom or dad says, surprised, "That's the old Bradlees where Nana Smith worked." The derelict store was the old Bradlees, with all the toys. I was a child the last time I saw her working there. I'd walked through the door swish, gone to my right, then left, the sections like a maze, and there she was with her piled-high hair, wearing a smock. It had seemed glamorous to me, her job: all those shelves and knowing where to stand, how to help, how to move through the aisles. She lived across the street and walked to work. She lived at 87 Howland Street, in a blood-red house. Old blood. The milky-nice cashier was walking in the aisles where she walked. That I walked as a child. I remember it in black-and-white, as if it was a movie.

The cashier gave us directions to a Home Depot, but I'd been looking at his kind eyes, not listening carefully to directions, and we wind up in dead end after dead end. We take the long drive back to Walmart. My parents wait in the car. "Don't take forever," my mom yells. I come from speedy people, but I am not speedy. They don't like waiting. It's hot for Massachusetts, muggy, and my father is sweating in the car. He likes the Cape, the breeze. We're too far inland for him. I buy beautiful yellow flowers still in their pot, very tall and happy. The cashier snips off the stalks that have died. She says, "It needs water." When I ask, "Do you have some?" she says, "Wait." The cashier reaches under the counter, fills up the bottle she drinks from, pours it in.

In the backseat of my parents' red car, shiny red of penny candy, I hold the pot of flowers on my lap, and the weight of it is like a child.

When I visit my son, I always put my fingertips inside the shamrocks carved in his stone. "Sweetest boy," I say. It's like touching the keyhole to a door I don't know how to open. I say, "Mom's here." If I were alone, I would lie down on the grass, over him. I would get as close and quiet as I can. But I don't want anyone else to see this. I can only pay attention when I'm unseen. So, I save the lying down for later.

The Shoe Museum is across the street from the mall, but in a dangerous, zigzaggy way that disturbs my parents. As we cross the road, my mom says my dad's name over and over in an escalating tone, without actually giving him any instructions. I shouldn't have dragged them here, but here we are. As we are greeted by the Shoe Museum director, I see why the place is closed for tours in the summer. It's July, and it seems as if it is at least a 120 degrees inside. No air-conditioning. No windows open. I have a few sips of water left in a bottle in my purse, but I get claustrophobic almost immediately. It's as though someone already breathed all the oxygen out of the air. They have no staff, only the director, a volunteer, who has opened the museum just for me.

The Shoe Museum director was the vice president of sales for Knapp Shoes and worked there for twenty-seven years. He's very tall. He shows me the lasts, each different shoe (and size) needing a new wooden last to shape the uppers and the soles on. I hold the red wood in my hand. There are lasts for the Duke Bill Shoe (1875), the Up-Swing Needle Toe Shoe (1885) with a toe like a scythe, the Ralston Shoe (1910) with seven pearl buttons in a Victorian arc, the Needle Toe Shoe (1880), lots more. He shows me the tiny decorative shoes, china shoes, celebrity shoes. He holds an ex-president's running shoe in the palm of his hand.

When he guides me upstairs to see old clothing that I have no interest in, the heat increases, rising to baking temperature in the attic. I wonder how he can continue to speak. I'm drenched. I've emptied the water bottle on my tongue. He is opening drawers full of scattered photos, pointing to outfits on hangers in a back room. "This isn't the ideal way to preserve things," he says, and I decide to bolt. I'm so thirsty, whatever I say to him sounds cottony. He follows me back downstairs. At the front door, leaving, it's my last chance to ask him what he knows. "Can you tell me about the skins for the shoes? Where the tanning took place?" A VP of sales—does he know where I'm going? He says that very few skins came from Brockton, though there were factories for all of the other auxiliary items, the lasts, etcetera. He says most of the skins came from Wisconsin, and Connecticut, I think, but not here. He's emphatic about that. When we shake hands, and he smiles, for the first time, I don't know what to say to him. He has two hearing aids, and as I go out the door, he says, "Where are you from again?"

On one of the summer trips back from the cemetery, I'd leaned over the front seat, like a child, rested my head between my parents, and told them the story of the kids with leukemia in Woburn. I told them about the toxic substance, trichloroethylene (TCE), found in the water. My dad said, "That's copy machine cleaner." He remembered it from the Navy. He'd been a storekeeper. I said, "TCE was used in tanneries. The lawyer said the tannery dumped TCE, and it went in the groundwater." My dad was quiet. He said, "All those shoes." We were all quiet. I hadn't thought it out before. A tannery treated skins, the skins made shoes. Brockton is the city of shoes. For hundreds of years. That's all my dad said, except, "I couldn't stand it if that kid died because we . . ." He said that. It still bugs me, the "we."

Migration

In 1969, two blind Siamese cats jump from one Formica counter to another in her kitchen. Nana Smith keeps every item in her house in exactly the same place, so the Siamese can find their way. She turns a key, peels a ham out of a tin, a pink body. "I like ham for Christmas," she says. I'm used to cooked food, an oven. The ham looks like something you'd eat during war or famine—meat that won't spoil. She has eyes like the blind Siamese, but bigger, blue glare, eyes that exclaim *what are doing what are doing, what's going on, what what!!* She's got the cats' restraint too. The Siamese want company; Nana Smith wants love.

In 1972, her second husband is in the living room, in a wheelchair, watching TV with his back to us. Sitting on the couch, we watch his back, but don't have a clear view of the TV show. He'd been hit by a car on his way to the mailbox. Tiring of us, he wheels down the dark hallway which seems like a way out, a mysterious road, but probably leads to a tiny bedroom, more quiet. He never spoke to me, never looked me in the face. Now he shares a gravestone with my son, is in fact buried beside him. They share the same name. The man in the wheelchair is the father of my uncle, my son's adoptive father.

In 1977, when we live on a military base in southern Spain, Mom's already bought a bottle of Dry Sack for Nana Smith as a

Christmas present. The bottle so uniformly dark it could be ink inside or blood. My brother and I aren't allowed to drink, but we'd gone to the bodegas on a tour, with Mom. We drank the tiny sample bottles of sherry in the cellars we visited, no drinking age here, and Mom didn't stop us. I felt her go with the flow. My dad looked at Nana's Dry Sack. "She can't drink. Why give her that?"

My mom says, "We always do it. She likes it." My dad shakes his head. "Then, what do we get her? What does she like?" My parents bought her a porcelain sailor boy, a Lladró figurine. A boy with downcast eyes and white pants that look like thick white tights, who carries a ship at his hip.

In 1979, Nana Smith lives on Howland Street when I am in my first year of college at Bridgewater State College, my parents overseas. She has me over, and opens the door to her bedroom. It's all pink. Familiar, like my pink canopy bed at home, but overwhelmingly girly. "Here's a light for you," she says, switching on a table lamp. The edge of shade, bedding, curtains—everything in the room—feels lacy. She says, "I never wear foundation. It ruins your skin." I don't know where she sleeps.

While I'm at Bridgewater, my aunt Julia and uncle Mark, who will adopt my son in two and a half years, take me out to dinner with Nana. In the restaurant, she orders a Shirley Temple. Puts her fingers in the watery grenadine, pulls out a cherry. "I can have a drink," she says. "One drink. I had one drink the other day." She's trying to convince my aunt and uncle she can handle a real drink.

After my son died, Nana came to Florida for a visit. She asked me why no one in our house talks about him. "I'd go crazy if I didn't talk about him," she said. The hallway is very narrow, and I can breathe the powder on her face. "I have a picture of him in my wallet. He looks just like you," she said. She opens her purse and shows me the two babies, one photo in black-and-white, flip, Tommy in color. Me and my son. "Here, you take them," she said.

Turning out the bathroom light, she said, "If you fall in love again, go on the pill."

In 1986, Nana sends me a gift: two black Siamese cat sculptures with green eyes. I lost one or broke it or threw it away. The other is at the foot of my bed. Once I was kind to her, thoughtful of her love for pretty things. The way she'd save the bag that held what you'd given her. Hang it from the back of her bathroom door. I'd gone to the mall, and in The Limited, a store where I thought almost exclusively of myself, I had twenty dollars. I bought Nana Smith a silver necklace with a pendant. I saw her wear it once, bright on her chest, on her sweater. Her sisters were circling her in the house. I could tell that she knew that it meant she was loved. Years later, when she dies, her jewelry is found in the cardboard Limited box with the black top. Emptied of the necklace.

In 1998, after my grandmother on the Cape dies, I visit Nana in a massive, low-income building in Brockton, in her LEGO-like apartment. I want her to act like a grandmother. I want her to say, "I'm sorry your nana died," and touch my hair. She brings two dresses out of her closet, says, "I bought them from a catalog." She's pleased with herself. The dresses look like triangles. "Are you mad at me?" she asks.

Soon, Nana starts refusing everything—food, TV, conversation, books. Soon she'll run away and then be kicked out of this assisted living home. She'll retreat completely into herself in a mental hospital, die two weeks before I arrive. But in the home, I've brought her a photo found in an attic in Ireland, of Nana Smith and my dad, as a baby. And another photo of her just married to Ben Groom and pregnant with Frank O'Connor's son (my dad), and nobody knows this but her, not the men, not her half sister, Anne, who knows everything. She wears a beret, and looks slightly drunk but delicate. Ben behind her, not looking at the camera, as if he can't believe his luck, what he's done. She looks wild, as though she is a quiet animal in clothes. She leans one way, he another, so that the house behind them seems to tip. "It's you," I say.

After she dies, I drive to Rockland to find her grave. I don't know this city, the streets intravenous. The only familiarity is a drugstore chain. "Where is Holy Family?" I ask the cashier at the CVS store. She doesn't know. The man in green pants in the aisle doesn't know.

The cashier says, "My dad will know." She takes out her cell phone. I follow her out into the parking lot while she talks. It's empty, a gray arena where something used to happen. It turns out Nana's cemetery is nearby—it's like one big roundabout. Inside the cemetery gate, I call my dad.

"I'm here," I say. "Where do I go?" I can tell he's surprised that I've found the cemetery, that I'm near his mother. I can hear that he is surprised to have a daughter who will find his mother. Who brings her flowers.

Once I saw an animal, a llama, just after she gave birth. I'd happened on her, in a clearing of a nearly deserted safari park where the animals come toward you in your car, as if they're departing Noah's Ark: camels, elk, wildebeests, pigs, deer, buffalo. Everyone hungry. There aren't enough visitors with white buckets of feed to hold out their open windows. The animals swarm us, flies on their hides. Dark eye after dark eye pressed to the window I refuse to roll down. But my friend in the backseat is interested in migration, the way things come toward us. He takes picture after picture—the ostrich stretching his iridescent blue neck behind my own, blinking so fast he seems not to blink. The fawns with their blond eyelashes lifting their heads up, toward us, too small to see. I turn around in my seat to see the black nose of a buffalo wet against my friend's knuckles. "Or," he asks, "is migration when they go away? Should I photograph them coming or going?"

He's the one who first saw the mother and her baby. The back of the mother llama bright red with blood from the birth we'd missed by seconds. But she is casual, still standing. The baby mostly bones and loose flesh, like a bird the way it lifts its front legs and falls. Lifts from the back and falls. Flesh like wings spread out on the ground. A small crying sound from the baby is the only noise. Once or twice, the mother bends her head to the baby. Then she sits down, close by, and lets the baby struggle. When it's time for us to move on, I'm sorry to leave before the baby can stand. Before that struggle ends. But a woman in a van in front of us had stopped as well. She leans out of a window, as if from a house. Her shirt pink. She's transfixed by the llama baby's effort to stand, but as we pass, I meet her eye. She smiles at me like a mother, as though she recognizes me.

In the Rockland cemetery, I take a few turns marked by other stones, other deaths, and I'm there. "I'm here," I say. I leave a mum on her stone, cream-colored like a wedding dress, and pink flowers above her grave grass, like a little trellis, tell her, "I'm not mad." I tell her she was perfect, which isn't true. I mean, I'm sorry that I punished her for resembling me. Afraid the pattern of her helpless life was bred into my genes. Her childishness and passivity. Both of us unmarried, pregnant teenagers. Nana apparently never telling my dad's father she was pregnant. Marrying another man instead. Her secrecy. Her selfishness in abandoning her kids to the orphanage and to relatives. If she's selfish, am I selfish too? I never asked her why she left her children. It seemed as though she couldn't grow up. As if she'd been hurt so much as a child— mother dead, father discarding her—she stayed a child, trying to find someone to take care of her. I used to walk around the lake at night, look at the light in the houses, wish someone would take me in. It reminds me of Nana telling my dad at seventeen years old that he needed to support her and the rest of the family. I wish she could have grown up. I would like to have known who she was under all that fear. She's been dead a year, Nana. Grass grown over, but her name's not carved into the stone. The only way to know she's here is to remember her.

How to Make a Shoe

The shoe is a kind of body. It has an anatomy. Throat, tongue. Vamp, a feather line, shank, heel, welt. The welt has a flesh side into which the sewing goes. A last is the model made for every shoe, every size, like a wooden foot. A puppet foot. At night, I'd run beside the city of shoes, the city where I was born. I wore my first pair of running shoes, bought by my grandmother. Before that I had shin splints, a burning that lifted only when I ran again, in my tennis shoes, so thin I could feel the sidewalk on my soles, tiny pebbles. At school I limped from class to class.

But in my running shoes, in my first year of college, I ran until I ran out of breath. Years before, Rocky Marciano, the undefeated champion boxer, had run a few miles away, in 1950s Brockton, in black boots. Black leather training shoes made on a Muson Military last. They look like war boots. Size 10.5. Heavy, double leather soles. He ran 750 miles in those shoes. Eight-inch blucher pattern with a straight tip: a high shoe with laces over the tongue, modeled after a half boot. To the shins. Open throat. The Rock from Brockton.

I'd leave at midnight to run, a girl in my dorm warning me once against it. When another girl teased her for sounding parental, she said, "Someone has to be a mother." I wanted quiet, darkness. I'd run past a factory and look up at the dark windows, feel the charge of someone looking out or bent over a table at a task, someone gone. The dust of their being there. Like when they dig up the ground and find city after city, one layer on top of another. Time right in front of me, inside the brick and the air, the soul of the world.

The day my son was born was the same day that Rocky began his professional career as a boxer. Thirty-four years later. I'm not saying my life's tied to his, not saying my son's life is tied. But we intersect like a body, something stitched together. Once, Rocky almost drove over my father's foot with his car, coming to a halt at the drugstore in Brockton. My father, a child then, jumped back. Rocky said something: "Hey, kid." Rocky died in a plane crash in Iowa. He was retired, hosting a weekly boxing show. Going home to his wife for his forty-sixth birthday party. But he's buried near me now—Forest Lawn Memorial Cemetery in Fort Lauderdale, Florida—a ride slightly south on the map.

A shoe is mapped. The bottom has an inner sole, a filling like granulated cork. A welt's a narrow strip of leather sewn to the rib. A sandal has a runner. The sole (leather, pure rubber, resin rubber, or plastic) and heel (nailed or stuck, Cuban, Louis, or wedge), heel lifts, top piece (the walking surface of a heel), toe puff: a reproduction of the toe of the last. Stiffener, shank (metal or wood to reinforce the waist), sock (inserted into the completed shoe with the maker's name), and eyelets. Hobnail shoes had a short nail hammered into the sole for durability. Sometimes, the nails were placed in a pattern, sometimes the nails spelled words to be left in the ground as a shoe print. A message you could leave behind.

I was seventeen when I went to Bridgewater State College in Massachusetts, after spending almost my whole life on other coasts. But I'd lived the first year of my life in the town next door, Whitman. When I was born, I came home to the apartment, steep second-story, gray. A salesman had come to the door and sold my mom a stroller that converted into a high chair, and a carriage, and a child's Formica and chrome table. All in one. She said that when I rode in it, I was the Queen of the Neighborhood. There was a tiny bathroom with no bath. A galvanized tub in the bedroom. On a map, Bridgewater and Whitman are connected by seams with the city next door, Brockton. I was born in Brockton, and my son is buried there. Sewn together.

In 1900, there were ninety shoe factories in Brockton. The Charles A. Eaton Company was in operation then, a shoe factory on Centre Street. It's just been converted into lofts. I want to get in. But there's no parking, the building right on the street. I get a machine when I call the sales office. I'd stroll around it, but it's not a strolling kind of place, few pedestrians. No stores. *The Boston Phoenix* called the city of my birth *a violence-prone, run-down hole.* There's a plaza I drive through, lost, a white square. Plazas remind me of the women in Argentina who held placards with photos of their missing children, abducted, disappeared under the military dictatorship between 1976 and 1983. The Mothers of the Plaza de Mayo. Now in that Buenos Aires plaza, there is a white shawl painted on the ground.

Centre Street takes me to Cary, where I'm hoping to find Calvary, my son's cemetery with its name spelled out in white stones on a hill. It's the first time I've tried to find it by myself. But I've turned too soon, into St. Patrick's, where only two men walk, two children. One man says, "No one's been buried here for fifty years." I feel as though I've woken in the future. Driving down Centre Street again, lost, I stop at a pink and brown Dunkin' Donuts, but the cashier doesn't know Cary Street, doesn't live here. I've never been able to find my way. Drinking coffee in the parking lot, a circle of air around me, no other cars. It feels like an abandoned land. There's a blue cross on a building to my right, a hospital,

Brockton Hospital. Where I was born. When I first saw the world outside, I saw this: Centre Street.

I find the grave without flowers. My child in my arms and then, my arms empty. I sit at his grave, his body under the grass in my hands. I talk to him as I did the day he was born. In the rocking chair, before the nurses knew he'd be adopted, after they'd made the beautiful mistake of giving him to me. I can still feel the weight of him. His calm in my arms.

When he died from leukemia, I would think about breast-feeding. That if I'd breast-fed him, he'd have had the natural protection it gives. That it would have given him protection against this city where he died. A city of shoes for two hundred years. What did that do to the water quality?

I don't know what was in the water when my son was born, lived here, and died. I don't know if my decision to give him away killed him. Before he was born, I remember looking forward to getting in shape. Then I was bleeding in the shower at the hospital—a shower room at night, the nurses at their stations near small circles of yellow light, my uterus not contracting though I kneaded it with my knuckles. I could hardly stand, naked, blood everywhere. This is how my great-grandmother died, childbirth, in Rockland—another town next door to Brockton. Her name so close to mine, Nelly. Afterward, her children were strewn apart. Nana Smith became a kind of slave, forever lost and childlike, giving her own children away, as I did mine. When I handed my son over, he cried the whole way out. I heard him in the garage, a shoe box attached to the house. I heard him in the car. I hadn't known my arms would feel stripped down the insides, where our bodies had touched on the outside.

Once I met a woman from another country who came to Florida: Ana. Years before, her brother had died, disappeared on a cruise ship here. She rode a bus to Miami with her video camera.

When she returned to my town, she played images of ships in port, a nightclub with people passing by. She was looking for her brother. Ana had come to say good-bye. I'd never met her brother, but in the face of a boy walking by the camera, the red square of light, I saw the absence of him. I saw how much the evidence meant. The solidity of things, the air where he'd walked.

I need to know the parts of the body to make a shoe, how it's sewn together. The elementary shoe has three basic parts: the vamp, quarters, and topline. All shoes fall into seven basic types: moccasin, sandal, mule, clog, boot, pump, and oxford. But the fashion wears me down—the silk damask, the French pump. What did the poor wear, the working class? The dead? Coffined in their dress shoes? Who wears rosettes? Men's embroidered velvet shoes? I need the basics. What did my son wear? Did you save a lock of his hair? Is there a baby book of first things? I can't ask my relatives these questions. I take three photos of an abandoned shoe factory on Church Street in Rockland. Beautiful red brick, hundreds of small windows laid out like cards, broken where something was thrown. The windows in the factory could be a calendar with a square for each day, the size of a postage stamp already cut, so all you have to do is lift it up to see inside. You could walk right in. I can't hold anything tangible: the blue sleepers I bought him, a rattle, a toy, anything he touched, except me. When I look in the mirror I see him in my face. But I'm not here to say good-bye. I did that once. I'm here to say hello. I'm here for evidence. The first shoe that was just a braid of grass. Leaves people wore on their feet. The shoes that are magical in stories and supposed to bring luck.

Hotline

A little more than a year before I get pregnant, when I'm in my first year of college in Massachusetts, my aunt Julia and uncle Mark take me to a party with relatives I don't know. It's the fall of 1978. I keep hearing people say that I'm my father's girl. It's strange and comforting to be identified that way, a girl belonging to someone. I walk between their bodies like shadows wearing color. I feel like a facsimile, carry a glass in my hand. "Hello," I say to strangers who are related to me somehow, who look for my father in my face. I'm living in a shared dorm room on a hill. Bridgewater is a teacher's college that began in 1840, in one room of the town hall basement. My roommate from Salem disapproves of my clothing. Her shirts are long-sleeved, buttoned high; even through her thick sweaters, she sweats dark circles. She throws her arms behind her head, cradles her skull. Lonesome for Salem, she lasts only one semester. I imagine her town full of witches, dark hair.

I do not want to become a teacher. But my mother graduated from this school, and my family is still living in Spain, so this school seemed a safe choice. A thin, dark-haired woman speaks to me at the party. I have to look down. If we're related, I don't know how. She works in social services, and tells me about an off-campus suicide prevention hotline training class. It's an eight-week course that certifies participants to work the hotline in town. I've been thinking of calling the Samaritans myself, the hotline in Boston. But I could go to this class instead. I can learn from both the expert and the sick how not to kill myself.

A few days later, I wander into the building that houses the hotline, ready to sign up for the class. It's like a barn, high-ceilinged with lots of open space. There's a desk, table, but little other furniture. A strange man with wolf hair signs me up and asks me out. He buys me wine that is too sweet, like alcoholic Kool-Aid. One night we are in a room with a bed, a quilt. He has the stomach of a beer drinker and heavy eater. An old man. But he's young and confident that I am attracted to him, though I'm both repelled and drawn to him in a weird, somnolent way. I detach myself from the magnetic pull of revulsion and passivity—and I can hear him behind me, confused at my walking away on the wood floor.

When I show up for the actual suicide class, it's in a cafeteria. Kitchen closed for the night. We all face front and listen. Each week we role-play with a partner. I turn my chair and face a social worker in training. The other students are here for college credit and see me as a volunteer, someone here simply because of an interest in helping others. The first night, I meet Nicole. When I tell her that I'm seventeen, she says, "If you need someone to buy for you, I can." This is great news. I hate standing outside the liquor store in the dark with my money in my hand, trying to hand it to strangers, to convince someone to buy a bottle for me. "Do you want to get high?" Nicole asks. Of course, of course I do. She lives in Wood Dorm, with a girl who's being kicked out of school in a few days. A promising group. The room is full of smoke. It's relaxing. Three girls share this tiny room. I'll meet Holly, the third girl, the next time I visit. She's beautiful with sleepy, kind eyes. Holly finds friendly roommates for me to live with in her dorm, loans me her clothes, sets me up with her boyfriend's best friend. There's no meanness in her.

The room has a bunk bed, one twin. Nicole's hair is red, messy. She's a little overweight, but bigger-boned than me. At meals, she eats with her head close to her plate as if she can't see her food. Her glasses are so thick they make her eyes look blurry, far away. She's twenty-one. Sometimes she loses her mind—throwing everything in the room up in the air. All her belongings, all her roommates' things. Anything left out flies to a new place. Holly's even-keeled. When she comes home after one of Nicole's fits, it's the only time she raises her voice. I think the rooms are too small, all that sitting there looking at each other like animals in a zoo.

It's snowing when I leave Nicole's room that first night. Snow lands in my hair. I'm happy to have a friend, a source for alcohol, place of welcome where I can get high. I'm the only person walking on the long road through the campus, up the high hill to my dorm. The police car behind me is at odds with my fog. I ignore it, keep walking. "Hello," the cop says, driving along beside me. "Would you like a ride?"

"No," I say. I know that I must smell like pot, that I have been enveloped in it, my hair full of smoky molecules. The cop insists. The night is cold and late. I sit in the backseat like a mild criminal, but he could be a kind cabdriver. The car's warmth quilt-like, and I forget to be on edge. I don't know how things work here. What the real crimes are. The Bridgewater Correctional Complex, a state prison, is nearby. The prisoners and the students both housed in multistoried buildings. When I go running down the hill at night, the great winding hill that leads to town, and look up at the rise on the other side, I imagine the prisoners. I think one is out there in the dark with me. Our bodies try to get away.

In addition to the prison and the college, the town has a Friendly's restaurant, Dunkin' Donuts, a record store that smells purple, liquor store, convenience store, and a clothing shop. Everyone seems to dress the same: muted and neat in their square-edged pants and shirts. After eight weeks, I complete the suicide prevention hotline course. I've missed a couple of classes, but the instructor hands me a printed certificate. I could frame it. I don't know much about preventing suicide. Nicole is going to sign up to work the crisis hotline. It's not just for suicide—there is a Rolodex of referral information for other things like birth control, pregnancy. But suicide gets handled in-house. You have to work the hotline in pairs. So Nicole asks if I want to pair with her.

On our hotline night, we stop at the liquor store. Nicole buys a bottle of Kahlúa. In the convenience store, she buys milk. Nicole has the key to the hotline building. It's just us in the barnlike rooms. We walk upstairs. Set up our drinks. "Go buy us subs at the store," Nicole says. So I do. I've never bought a sub before.

The person behind the counter asks, "What do you want on it?" I don't know.

I say, "Nothing." Unwrapping her sandwich, Nicole is disgusted.

"What? Nothing? Haven't you ever gotten a sub before?" She eats her cheese and meat sandwich dry. In Spain there was a snack shop on the base that sold hoagies. I realize a hoagie is a sub. America feels confusing. It feels fast after Spain, the buildings higher. One night Nicole and I are on duty, and it's still early, the phone rings. I'm just starting to get drunk. We take turns answering the phone. It's my turn, so Nicole nods at me. All I've done so far is flip the Rolodex, give out phone numbers in a helpful tone of voice. On the phone, a man says, "Who are you?" He tells me that he's going to kill himself unless he can come to the hotline house to talk to me. He sounds a little bit like he's flirting. As though he wants to go out on a date with me. A talking-about-suicide date.

I fling the phone at Nicole, the professional, the counselor-to-be. She smirks at me. She knows I can't handle the mentally ill. Later, she'll laugh at my cracking, the panicked black receiver in the air between us. But she catches it, and her voice is cool and clinical. She sounds like a nurse. Nicole knows how to save a life. I eat my sub. Drink my Black Russian. I can't hold the class material in my head. I need a bulleted list, concrete instructions. Maybe I should have raised my hand. Asked a question. I was so worried that my real reason for being in the class would be discovered, I said almost nothing. Simply talking to a stranger, in person or on the phone, was so anxiety-producing, it took almost all my wherewithal just to see or hear them.

Nicole and I have a fight one night. She sits in a chair in her crowded dorm room at three in the morning, drunk and ripe for fit pitching. My closest friend at school furious with me, so I jump up. Head for the door. Nicole sees the shift immediately and says, "Don't let Kelle out." Nicole throws her body like some agricultural project against the wooden door—her red hay hair, milky limbs, udderlike breasts. Big as she is, she's soft like blankets, unexercised. It isn't hard to push her out of the way. I have the idea to throw myself in front of a car. Thinking nothing of the driver, killing or maiming a girl, a drunk minor. Once I'm outside with snow on me, I calm down. The approaching car is very slow. Everything slows down. Nicole sends my boyfriend after me. Burgess. He and I have so little conversation, so little in common. Our communication is only physical. But his hair shines; he comes after me. A town boy who puts his arms around me like snow in the snow.

Arabia

1.

The summer of 2006, my parents and I go to the house of my grandmother's half sister, Anne, in Brockton. Anne can't talk. I noticed this on the phone, when I'd called her in 2003, asked to visit Nana Smith—the long gaps between her words, as if she were on an overseas phone call.

Now she can't swallow very well either. The muscles in her throat have become mysteriously paralyzed. I spend the night with her alone. She had seemed the stable sister, the one I could count on to tell me about Brockton, Nana Smith, Tommy. But I waited too long, and now she can't talk. It's like a hideous mystery from one of those Ripley's Believe It or Not comics. The frozen woman. Watching her pour water in the coffeemaker, her hand shaking, I start to cry. But Anne is unnervingly self-sufficient. She doesn't complain about anything and doesn't want tears. She lives alone with her cat, cooks, drives. You'd think she had some minor complaint. "Can I help?" I ask. She points to a cupboard, cups and saucers.

Anne must wonder why I'm here. Staying with her for the first time. She writes me a warning, in pen on yellow notepaper: "Don't be disturbed by the way I drink coffee. Sometimes the coffee bursts out." Her napkin gets stained. Once she lived in Arabia, and she shows me all the charms on her bracelet: slipper and mosque, a ruin in Lebanon ("a beautiful ruin," she writes), a pyramid, a carriage with tiny turning wheels, an oil rig—carrying the places she went on her wrist, in gold. In Arabia, Anne said, she wasn't allowed to speak to any Arabs, men or women. I asked, "How did you buy anything?" And she said, "Brad had to buy everything." She tried to speak to the gardener one time, and he never came back.

Anne asks if I want to go to the cemetery, Tommy's grave, and I say yes. But she gets lost driving me there. "It's okay," I say. "I don't have to go today." We pass a woman in a shiny pink skirt to her knees, walking in a gully. I'm nervous about Anne driving, the paralysis, but it seems she drives everywhere. Takes her friend on museum trips to Boston. Anne's doctor is concerned she'll need a feeding tube soon. It would fit inside her, below her ribs, and then she wouldn't be drinking or eating anything. I'm worried that everything inside her will freeze, like her throat, the drool clear and constant now, like a baby's. What happens if her lungs freeze? Her heart?

There's a library upstairs, and at night, we sit in big chairs surrounded by books. Tell me about my son, I want to say. How was Nana Smith with my son, watching him all day, every workday? Taking care of him. My grandmother who'd given her own children away for a time, who was given away herself by her father. Anne said my grandmother was innocent all her life. When she was pregnant with my dad, Nana Smith asked Ben Groom's sister how the baby would come out. Ben's sister said, "The same way it got in."

Anne didn't actually say it. In addition to the yellow notepad, she has a small keyboard with a lit-up screen for longer conversations. She types what she wants to say, and it appears in green letters on the two-sided screen, so that you could sit across the table from her and read what she's thinking. She can also press the audio button when she's done, and an electronic voice, female, speaks for her.

Anne says that when my son died, "That's when Gertrude started losing her memory." What was it like for Nana Smith to be given away, her mother dead, father remarried? And for a time, Nana Smith was like a servant in their house, unwanted by the new wife. I know Nana didn't attend her high school graduation because she didn't have a dress. I know she worked and bought little things for Anne. Nana's body in Holy Family Cemetery now, on Center Street in Rockland. The ground just cut, the shape of the hole for her coffin. It's hard to think of her body in the ground. She was so pretty, her delicate face, fine nose, chin held up, her bedroom all pink. So badly married, like Queen Gertrude.

When my parents had dropped me off at Anne's house, the front door had been open, so my parents and I walked inside. My mother and father and I sat on Anne's couch in the darkened room. It was as if we'd entered a house where no one lived. As Anne came silently down the stairs and entered the living room, my mom said to her, "You looked like a ghost." Maybe it was the quiet, her inability to speak.

In the library that night, she'd given me a book about one of my favorite painters. I hadn't read it yet, but after the paralysis took over Anne's body and she'd been placed in a facility, after my father called to say she weighed seventy pounds and was curled up in bed like a broken finger, waiting to die, only her eyes working—haunting, he said, just staring at him—I looked for her book. Inside she'd inscribed it on July 17, 2006: "Kelle, with much love and more understanding. Anne." When I flip through the book, a photo falls out. It's Nana Smith wearing a black coat with leopard-print collar standing next to Anne, who looks about thirty, smiling, pretty in a white sweater.

2.

At lunch, I don't give Anne enough eye contact. She's driven me to see Mark and Julia. We've met at a restaurant. After lunch, on the open porch at my aunt and uncle's new house, I learn that Julia not only worked as a secretary for the Knapp Shoe Factory, but also for the Shoe Museum director. Julia said, "Oh, he was the boss of the managers I worked for." She walks to the beach at the end of the road with me.

A wide beach, as though the ocean is opening. Blue metal tiles under my feet lead out into the water, over the rocks to the clear sandbar. When we have to go single file through the dune, Julia is in front of me. I can't see her face, so I ask her, "Some time, can we talk about Tommy?" It's the first time we've mentioned his name to each other since Julia took him in her arms from the house in Orlando when he was four days old. She's quiet at first. Then she faces me, says something about not knowing if I blamed them. She says, "I had no one to talk to after he died. Mark couldn't talk about it." She says that it was very cloudy the day they buried my son.

"Gloomy." After they put his body in the ground, she says, the sun came out and filled the sky. She smiles at me.

"What did he like?" I ask.

"He was too young to like things. He was just a baby," she says.

What does she think I mean? I don't mean did he like baseball or what was his favorite TV show. Did he like blue? Did he like a song? I remember once someone said he liked Cheerios. Either Nana Smith or Dad told me that, when he went to visit Tommy at Easter, right before he died. He liked Cheerios and the petals on pink carnations. But I can't push Julia. She's the one who took care of him, fed him, played with him every day, watched him die. She put his body in the ground. Had to let them cover him up and walk away. Go back home. I wonder what a person can do after that. What can ever matter? I think that any attempt at happiness—to see a movie or sing along to the radio, anything she's been able to do—is brave. She walks beside me, puts her hand on my back. I do the same for her. It's something a mother would do, I think. It's a little awkward to walk like this—we're tippy. "He'd be . . ." she says, calculating his age. As if she'd been keeping him somewhere, the memory of a baby, and now she can see him rising up, grown, in front of us. I can see he's tall now, the way she's looking up.

Hour of Death

I asked for my son's death certificate today. He died twenty-five years ago. It's almost Christmas 2007. I'm living alone in a glass cabin in New Smyrna Beach, Florida. The artists' residency center where I work closes down for a winter break. It's the same place I came to in 1993, when I did a residency for three weeks. I'd been so happy here. So, in late 2005, I'd contacted the director, asked her about a position. She created one for me, and I'd moved to the coast in January 2006.

I've been renting a shared house on the ocean, and it's noisy. The downstairs neighbors have a party almost every night. I'd been warned that it would be too much for me, but I couldn't resist living in a house right on the beach. I could hear the ocean all night and day. Once the moon shone across the sea in a path that led right into my apartment, to me, where I slept on a futon in the living room. I thought, *who is waking me up?* It was the moon. I was so high up, that if I was seated in the living room, I couldn't see the shore. Just the water, as if my house was a boat, and I was floating.

But it's often hard to concentrate, and the residency center staff sympathizes, knows I need quiet to write. They've given me one of the artist cottages for a month, so I've combined my vacation time with the winter break. The cottage is surrounded by tropical jungle. Completely secluded. The only connection with the rest of the world is a winding boardwalk that leads to my door. Signs are posted that this area is private, but sometimes people can't help ignoring the signs. Then they see the small house, sun shading the windows. They walk up to the clear door, the floor-to-ceiling windows, cupping their hands around their eyes to peer in. Sometimes I wave. I like living so transparently in this old forest. On a preserve within another two hundred acres of preserved land. Here, there's nothing to hide.

At my desk in the cabin, looking out a wall of glass into the green leaves, I call Brockton City Hall and ask for the certificate. From Commercial Street, the east, City Hall rises out of the trees like a medieval fortress, a round tower with a steepled building rising higher in back, like a church. I'm ready to state my relation. To say, "I'm his mother." And something shifts in my chest as if I'm jigsawed in there, a map of the world. A continent shifted to the right, toward the center. I felt like Rocky, like a pugilist, me who'd never hit anyone with anything except the gold buckle on my pink purse when I was seven in Honolulu. And the baby, the spanking, when I was eleven. I'm ready to say, "I'm his mother," to push in the glass doors, rifle the file cabinets. Demand this evidence.

But I'm on the phone. A clerk answers. I realize that I don't have to feel like a liar, as though I'm fabricating my relation to my son. I realize that as facts go, my saying, "I'm his mother," is absolutely true. But the clerk doesn't ask who I am. She says, "It's five dollars. Don't send cash." I mail her five dollars.

A few days later, the postman in Brockton stamps my envelope "Happy Holiday." The city clerk had put the Certificate of Death inside. A yellow paper. Name: Thomas Edward Smith. Date of Death: May 27, 1982. Age—Last Birthday: 1.

There is a box next to this one that says "Under 1 Year" with one box underneath for Months, one for Days. Next to this is another box that says "Under 1 Day" with a box for Hours, a box for Minutes. For those who lived for Minutes.

In the box, "If U.S. War Veteran Specify War," someone has written "No." "Immediate Cause" is in two parts: A and B. B is "Acute Myelomonocytic Leukemia." "Interval between onset and death: 5¾ mo." A is "Respiratory Arrest." "Interval between onset and death: 1 min." Hour of Death: 5:30 p.m.

The doctor, Beth Gleghorn, signed this form the day he died, her handwriting nearly unreadable. I wonder if it was sadness in her hand or if she always wrote like this. I'd like to do a handwriting analysis of Beth Gleghorn.

Place of Death: Boston. County of Death: Suffolk. Hospital: Tufts N.E. Medical Center 2299. In the Devonian Period, mountains were raised here. Fish got jaws. Large trees appeared. One minute nothing, a million years later, there are sharks and bugs and the trilobites die. The first birds flew.

When I go out for food, shopping in the grocery store, two women look at the orange juice; one says, "If I drink that I won't get drunk." They laugh. I meet the speaker's eye. She says, "I never drink," sounding drunk, tittery. Then a man says, "That's regular coffee," and a ponytailed man says, "I'm a regular guy." An overweight man in a bathing suit tells me, "You should get goggles." I have goggles. They help me breathe. I can see where I'm going.

1982

One hand wrote in a black, felt-tip pen across the blank back side of an index card, "Adriamycin," in very good cursive, a steady hand. Below the *n* is another hand, a red pen, younger like a high school girl's, round: "1982." The 9 has been corrected, an 8 hidden underneath, as if the person writing was having trouble knowing what century it was. Beneath the year, in red again: "Jan 1, 2, 3." Below this is whiteness. Midway down the card, the emptiness is interrupted by a red line of ink separating the top from the bottom. Right beneath the line, in the same red hand: "GT.G." The period after the first *G* forgotten. A space, then: "—pill"

Underneath this line is only a small space, and then: "2/25—"

In 2007, I put the information together as carefully as I can. This is what I know of my son's treatment for leukemia. I know that in December 1981, he had bruises, but had not fallen. He was nine months old. I know that he got the leukemia into remission, and it went into his spine. I know that he got the spinal cancer into remission, and it went into his brain. I know that the doctor said they would give him one last treatment, but that if the bump on his head didn't shrink, they wouldn't do any more treatments, that it would make things worse. I think that he died in my uncle's arms on May 27, 1982, in Children's Hospital in Boston. But in December 2007, I received the death certificate. Twenty-five years after my son died, I learned that he died in Tufts Medical Center. Everything I knew before, I'd only overheard, guessed. I could never ask anyone directly, "Where did my son die?" I'm finally able to ask.

The index card was in a red book that my father brought back with him from Brockton, when he went to see Tommy in April 1982. When my relatives told my dad he would need to come now. I remember my voice, my asking, like smoke, to go too. I didn't go. In a bar with my friend Sophie, I said, "He's not going to die." And Sophie said, "I know it's hard." She was wearing my red crocheted sweater. She said, "Look. He's a baby, he's got leukemia. It spread." Her face was tight. She wore purple lip gloss. The smoke was faintly suffocating. The room, an old train car, was warm. The band had gone on break, but the recorded music was loud enough that she had to raise her voice. She said, "Will you think about it for a minute?" She said, "Kelle, he'll die, sooner or later, he's going to die. Don't you see that?" I said, "You're wrong. Everyone's hopeful. The doctors, my relatives." Sophie said, "I know." We drank in the train car almost every night. When we didn't go, we missed it. Sometimes we went to drink at the Why Not first, so Sophie could look for the man with silver hair. He's the one who drove me home to my parents' house when I broke my foot at Sophie's holiday party, the year I gave Tommy away. Too old for her, but she'd had some kind of crush.

My dad came back home from Brockton with the red book, *You and Leukemia: A Day at a Time*, a freckled boy on the cover hugging a snowman. Inside was the index card. He brought back a photo of Tommy at home with my uncle. He'd just come home from the hospital. There were red lines drawn on his head, like a map. He was asleep in my uncle's arms. My uncle was leaning back on a couch, holding my son, smiling a little for the camera, smiling to have him in his arms. In another photo, Tommy is sitting on the lap of Nana Smith, and my aunt is beside him. An Easter basket is on Tommy's lap. Everyone is laughing. Something really funny has just happened. I think the person who took the picture has made them laugh. Tommy is so thin, he looks like a baby rescued from a concentration camp. His smile, though, is huge. It doesn't look like it could be any bigger, as if he couldn't be happier. The Easter basket means it's Easter, April. That he'll be dead at the end of May.

He has his first birthday in the hospital. March 17, 1982. When he was born, the nurse in the delivery room told me, "He'll have green birthday cakes the rest of his life." I don't know if he ever had a green birthday cake. But Nana Smith brought corned beef and cabbage to the hospital. She brought her best silverware. That's what I heard.

I read the red book. Adriamycin is a chemotherapy drug. They gave my son chemotherapy.

"Jan 1, 2, 3."

Are these the days he was given Adriamycin? It's given as an IV shot. Adriamycin, ADR, is an antibiotic. It stops cells from growing, so they can't divide. Stop cells from making DNA. It can hurt your heart if you get too much, but no one knows how much is too much. The red book says to tell your doctor if you have trouble breathing. Other side effects are nausea and vomiting, bone marrow depression, hair loss, sore mouth, burning pain where the needle went in if any ADR leaked out. The book says you will probably get only one or two of these. How does a baby tell his doctor he has trouble breathing?

Is your mouth sore? Let me kiss your sore mouth.

My dad said that Tommy was sick, vomiting, and my aunt was with him all the time. My dad said Tommy followed her everywhere.

The reason that there is no period after the first "G" in "G T.G."

is that the "G" is really a "6." The rounded handwriting confused me. "6-TG" is "6-Thioguanine." As it says on the index card, it's a pill. How did my aunt make the pill easy for him to swallow? It also stops cells from making DNA, so they can't divide. The side effects are bone marrow depression, loss of appetite, nausea and vomiting, and sore mouth.

There is nothing else on the card. There are no more cards. There is no handwriting in the book.

All I have is the red book. A woman with freckles holds the freckled boy on her lap. She's wearing bell bottoms. The boy has one arm around her shoulder, her neck. His mouth is a little O, so I know he is speaking. This page says, "All of us want to live a long time. And we want the people we love to live long lives." On another page, the freckled boy is bald. His mouth is an O again; he's talking to a girl in braids and knees socks. Behind her back, she holds one of her hands with the other. The red book says, "It's OK to be bald. Queen Elizabeth the First of England was bald, and she was a very great ruler." A baby doesn't care about being bald. He doesn't know what a ruler is.

To find out if you have leukemia, the doctor does a bone marrow aspiration, which looks a lot like a spinal tap. Black towel with a circle cut out. In the drawing, a child's diaper is held up with giant pins. The shinbone of the baby is shown, a dark rectangle on her leg. The book says that sometimes they use the shinbone in tiny babies. Is my baby a tiny baby? The book says, "You will have more bone marrows in the weeks, months, and years to come. Many people with leukemia think the bone marrow test is the worst thing about having leukemia. It hurts to have some bone marrow taken out of you." Aspiration is like "sucking it out through a thin straw." It hurts, the book says. Even though the boy's back is numbed. The baby is numbed. The book says that bone marrow "is even prettier than blood."

Another page is titled "Environmental Factors" and has a DNA model, a drawing of octagons, some black, some white, some dotted lines that connect octagons. The book says, "Most relatives of people with leukemia never get it themselves. Other things besides genetic factors must play a part in causing leukemia. These other things must come from the environment. All of these environmental factors have one thing in common: they can change the structure of DNA, and DNA is what your genes are made of. DNA contains the rules that your cells live by. All the environmental factors can change DNA, so they can probably change the rules."

Other things: radiation from an atomic bomb, chemicals, and viruses.

The book says, "Nobody caused your leukemia, nobody could have prevented it." I don't know what the book means.

On another page, the boy unzips himself.

Aortic

My male doctor puts two fingers from each hand in the valley of each of his hipbones, rests the pads of his fingers on the creases made by his tan Dockers. "Here are your ovaries," he says. I'm imagining my ovaries where his index fingers are. Imagine them shrinking from his fingers, the cotton. I'd thought this was just a precaution, going to a cancer doctor, walking past the chemo sign pointing to the right, happy with my best friend taking the time to accompany me. "You've got a fifty percent chance of ovarian cancer," he says to me. He's got my CT scan, blood work. Something drops from my throat into my stomach. "You have to have surgery now," he says, "as soon as we can schedule it."

When we leave his office, walk down the hall, the doctor is in a little alcove office with a nurse. He talks to the nurse about someone else as we pass by. "If she won't have the surgery, she'll die. Tell her she'll die." Long after this day, I'll realize he never said what other thing I might have from my symptoms: a stage 4 mass, elevated ovarian cancer test, enlarged aortic lymph node. The aortic news is its own terror because if there's cancer it means cutting me open to there, to my heart.

My friend must have done some talking to the doctor—we were in the room together. I remember when our smiling stopped, the smile still on my face but fear freezing it over. So shocked I forgot to stop smiling. Like when the manta rays came toward me in an invasion of black wings in the ocean, and my dad said, "Run," but I tried to act cool, go slow. For whom? The manta rays? The people on the beach? "Run!" my dad yelled.

My friend is the practical one. But I don't remember anything she said after the doctor said "fifty percent chance." Later, she showed me a poem she wrote about the visit, and it was all about my hair, how much she loved it. She was afraid I'd lose my hair; she'd lose me. It seems sweet, right? But I was mad. I thought, "Don't start eulogizing me. Don't chronicle my death." I love her; she's my dear friend, but I don't want this to be the beginning of my death. My death is not a poem. I thought of my son, how he'd had to turn toward the chemo sign, die. A baby. I think he is a thousand times more brave than me. I am afraid of pain, of what I've read of the treatment for leukemia, the hollow needle that sucks out bone marrow from the spine. My son was able to get the leukemia into remission, and then it turned to spinal cancer. And he got that into remission too. And then it went into his brain, and then people said, "He's only a baby."

He had a bump on his forehead like an orange, like the orange inside me. But his was cancer, and they couldn't get it to go away. I'm afraid of pain, of suffering, but I've talked to God, I've asked. I said if my child had any pain, give it to me. Give it to me. Let me take it. And I waited. But now I think that maybe there aren't any trades. That no one has to suffer to save another. And that if God has inscribed the name of my son on the palm of his hand, wouldn't he have kept him from hurting?

It's 2004, the year all four hurricanes come to Florida. I live at the top of a pink apartment building built in the 1940s. The roof right over my ceiling. Eighty-mile-an-hour winds tear the huge, ancient tree beside my dining room window out by the roots. I used to sit at my window to see the birds high up, at my elbow.

So that we really seemed to live in the same world. They weren't scared of me on the other side of the glass, playing their music. The tree falls sideways, along my building, rather than in, on me. Rather than turning my apartment into a room of flying glass. I'm afraid the roof will come off, and the delirium of Dorothy, of flying through the air, will be my death. I hide in the hallway between my rooms—close the bathroom, bedroom, living room doors. Crouch down. For once it seems stupid to be alone, with a dark machine ready to hurl me into the trees.

My surgery has to be rescheduled when the second hurricane is near. I drive to the coast, most of the beach sand washed away in the first storm. The national seashore empty, winter coming. I walk for miles without seeing anyone human. The sand strewn with boat boards and rusted nails, bottles, palm tree trunks, and when the tide comes in, it brings more. At high tide, there is nowhere to walk, boards flying toward me on the incoming waves. So I climb a little deck by a house abandoned to the vultures. And the water climbs around the deck, though I keep dry, until it seems as if I am on a boat myself, surrounded by water on three sides, dune on the other. And I feel safe there on the ocean. My heart stops panicking, stops imagining a knife, the cold cutting of my knit skin. Stops imagining chemo, what kind of burn that is. My hair on the floor like a recruit's. Soft body in a grave, under the dirt. Instead it seems as if the ocean reminds me of what remains. It carries me like an early relative from the first days.

Before the surgery, my heart beats so fast—like one of those little dogs that seem motorized, a hummingbird, some terribly quick thing. So both of my nurses compliment my hair, play with the curls. I feel the tenderness of their hands, their knowledge of my fear. And for once I don't pretend I want straight hair. "I like it too," I said. I want to keep it. I liked everything then—all the mysteriously named items inside me. The ones a nurse listed on a form, made me sign my permission that they could take any and all if I had cancer. So, I might wake up empty, not even knowing what I'd had to begin with. Emptied out like a suitcase. Even if I'm broken, I want them, I want all my broken things.

During surgery, the doctor calls my dad from the phone in the operating room. I'm still cut open on the table. My parents in the waiting room with my best friend. He said, "There's no cancer." In the waiting room, my dad calls my aunt and uncle, Julia and Mark, on his cell. "There's no cancer," he tells them. Julia cries.

When I start to wake up in the recovery room, a nurse is right beside my ear. I hear her whispering before I can see her, "There's no cancer." As if she wants her words to be the first thing I hear when I come to, so I don't have to wake up scared.

It turns out the manta rays, though related to sharks, aren't even dangerous. Toothless and acrobatic, they can fly through the air, but can't hurt you. The mass had been endometriosis, like a ball of yarn twined around my insides, wound to the size of an orange around my poor right ovary. So the doctor scooped it all out, took my strangled ovary too, sewed me up. The other symptoms were caused by all that twisting stuff, and after the surgery, go back to normal.

On the phone in the operating room, the doctor said, "I'll respect Kelle's wishes and not do a hysterectomy." I'd written the doctor a letter before my surgery. In the letter, I wrote, "If there's no cancer, I do not want a hysterectomy. I want to have another child." I'd thought a doctor would pay attention to something in writing, instead of my words in the air. I knew he thought that if I wasn't going to use my uterus, he'd want to spring clean me like a closet, send me into surgical menopause. But he'd listened to the letter.

I was forty-three years old, unmarried, and working in a homeless shelter. But I didn't have cancer, I wasn't dying, and I had one ovary left. One ovary is all you need to make a child. Once I was walking down a road in Virginia at three in the morning. The blue mountains were the same color as the night, light came from the stars and little roadside lanterns to my left. To my right, I felt the presence of a live being moving. It was two horses, hurrying to walk beside me, two dark horses keeping me company on their side of the fence. The hills all around me. Mostly I am insensible of trees, their states and bruises, their lack of disguise. Their willingness to reach out for the things that keep them alive.

Shelter

I'd fallen in love in 2001, quit my job. Got engaged and moved to New York. But it didn't work out, and by February of 2002, I was back in Orlando. Unemployed. The chimes left up in the wind outside my window sound like a dog constantly jangling its chain. Someone said the homeless shelter needed a new grant writer. During the interview, my license plate disappeared. At the front desk, the receptionist said, "You're late." I sat in a plastic chair in the waiting area for the homeless. A woman asked me, "Can't you get a better job than this?"

They buzzed me into the double doors. In the president's office, I don't tell him how close I am to homelessness myself. How my brother had given me rent money. So had a retired nun and her husband, and my sad boyfriend, and a temp agency. I've never worked for a social service agency before. He hires me anyway. Outside the president's window, we can see people gathered in the fenced-in picnic area. "What kind of relationship will I have with the clients?" I ask him.

"None," he said. "No interaction. Just focus on writing grants." Through the glass, one of the staff is holding a client's baby on his hip.

I don't want anyone to know I'm back in Orlando. The marriage off. So, I stay in my apartment except for work and a walk at night around the lake. I feel humiliated, foolish that I'd been so hopeful. Lonely. At the shelter, I have my own office the size of a closet, away from the administrative offices and my colleagues. I work where people live. At night, they line up in the hallway outside my door for dinner. Kids hop up and down to peek into my tiny window. People live behind me—I can hear a radio, feet kicking our shared wall. The clients' main entrance is just to the left of my office. The emergency rooms for victims of abuse and their kids are in another building, on another street. Those walls are white, the blankets, even the sky looks white—the kind of white you'd see from sudden pain, like a baseball hitting you in the face when tears aren't even there yet.

The help desk is at the end of the hallway, across from the staff bathroom. I'm waiting for someone to emerge from the storage closet behind the desk, so I can ask for hand soap. Beside me a baby girl who doesn't look old enough to be standing raises her hands up to me. She's covered in something sticky, all over her face, fingers. It looks like candy melted. But I'm grateful for the way she reaches up, as if I'm part of her family. Settled on my hip, she's so at ease. I could be a tree.

The only people who reach out to me, reach out their hands, are children. A lot of kids I only see a few times, but Tiny and her brother I see every day for six months. Every day, Tiny's brother stretches out his arm like a baseball player to clap my hand as if I've won something. Tiny gives me hugs, sometimes two a day. Once I was so low, and she's outside my door like a minuscule grandmother saying, "Give me a hug." She is two and a half years old when I meet her, her brother is seven. She gives me fashion advice (button my coat) and turns her stroller upside-down in the hallway to make a patient chair. She offers me a seat. When I plead my size, Tiny has me turn around like a model to see if I'm too big. I try to keep my distance, as the president asked, but one day

Tiny is in the fenced-in yard, caught up in pushing her stroller, when a need to pee catches her by surprise. On that gray concrete, the brightness looks like sun. But Tiny is stricken with humiliation and crying on one side of the fence, me on the other. Her father yells from a picnic table where he sits with several women. Finally her brother holds out his baseball-player hand to her and breaks the spell. After that, I bring a *Madeline* book for them, an against-the-rules gift, but when I find their case manager's office in a maze of rooms, she said the children and their family had left early that morning to look for another shelter. The parents hadn't worked their case plan, so the whole family was exited. Exited. Though, when I speak to the program director, corner her in the dining room that night, she lies, says, "They've been reunited with family." The case manager, Iris, said, "Tiny wouldn't let go of my neck." Like the day Tiny had dressed in her new white shirt, her hair in barrette curls, not wanting to go the doctor.

I'd last seen Tiny and her brother the night before. They were playing in the hall, and Tiny pushed on my stomach twice, gently, as if I was stuck, a kind of statue. Something she'd never done before. But she'd wanted me to play, to get going while there was still time.

With Tiny gone, I think I can't go back to work. She'd lived at the shelter for six months, there when I arrived. But in the morning, I take Parramore, past the men in wheelchairs with missing limbs, the woman who cries at the window of any car that stops at the red light. Past the small concrete building behind the grocery store that says in big red letters, NONE SHALL LACK. I pass the three hundred homeless men who mill on the street after leaving the metal Men's Pavilion. They get a meal, spend the night on the floor. Each man gets a parking spot—a human-length rectangle painted in white on concrete, and a bright blue sleeping pad that fits inside the lines. The parking lot is full of pee streams from homeless men who don't want to wait in line for the bathroom. Urine like a cloud in my throat.

Another day, at the clients' reception desk I was going to ask to be buzzed in, but a woman is talking to the receptionist. Her baby sits on the counter, Josiah. He is so beautiful, I have to say hello. Josiah, a King of Judah in the seventh century BC. Josiah, meaning *the Lord supports.* Later, there is a fire alarm, and I hold him in my arms. It is what I want most, to hold a baby in my arms. No one here is afraid of my brokenness—everyone so shattered, no one even sees it. When I hold the baby, it's as if everything inside me is blanketed with light. I stop echoing and sputtering, and shaking. He stops crying when I speak to him, looks into my eyes. A thoughtful king, listening.

On my first day at the shelter, the program manager opens the door to my office. My desk doesn't have any drawers. No writing utensils. No wastebasket. Filthy air vent overhead. The building is an old television station from the 1950s. Cramped and mazy. The small offices could sleep up to two families. No windows. No fresh air.

When I meet the first girl, she is walking in the hallway with her belongings in a plastic bag. Three or four years old. She hears my door click closed, and turns around, asks, "Where are you going?"

And I say, "Home," her dad up ahead, waiting for her to catch up so they can go through the doors to the family rooms. The girl blew me a kiss. I blew one back. Mine takes a few seconds. She touches her cheek, surprised. I don't hear her name when she says it and am embarrassed to ask again. As if I'm at a cocktail party, so afraid of forgetting my own name that I don't hear anyone else's. Forgetting she's three years old and has been pretty forgiving.

Nefertiti in the Head Start trailer had earned her name. Regal, straight-backed in her chair, head half-turned toward me while the other kids sing three songs in a row. Shining, quiet, Nefertiti holds out her hand to pull me down to sit on the carpet. Demands I listen to her read me a story.

To make photocopies, I have to go down the hall to the admin office. Every time I leave my office, I have to lock it. It's a lot of locking, unlocking. I'm fiddling with my keys when I see a boy barely old enough to walk, at the main door. My keys fly out of my hand as if he's called them. His mother's yellow and green muumuu is so bright I can't take my eyes off it. She said, "Did you make the lady nervous?" The boy starts to run toward me, which makes his mother laugh, "Go ahead, Moo Moo, give her a hug." He runs right into me, grabs my knees hard, like a post—the Lady of the Flying Keys.

When the half-assed air conditioner breaks completely, I have to keep my door open to breathe. A girl floats in, asks, "Do you have any candy?" The only bright object in my office is a Kleenex box with flowers, so she pulls one out like a scarf.

One day after work, in the parking lot I see the Boys & Girls Club lady standing with children and a man with a ringed pole, as if he's in a circus. He's come for the stray dog that lives here. But he can't find her puppies. The B&G lady asks, "Can't you take her later?" The stray has just given birth—she'd just been pregnant, and now is gaunt again. The puppies newborn; they need their mother. The B&G lady thinks the pups are under her portable building. She says, "It's going to smell if they die." But the maintenance guy says no, they've been calling Animal Control for two months, and every time, the stray disappears. The man with the ringed pole catches her then, screaming like any mother. Tosses her in the back of his trailer. He says something to the maintenance guy. The trailer so close, I can almost reach into the darkness, undo the ring around her throat.

The next morning, I walk by the B&G portable, listen for crying. One of the clients in the alcohol and drug treatment program, Michael, keeps walking the grass perimeter until he hears yelps. Another guy with jagged teeth crawls underneath the portable, in the dirt, scoops out nine puppies—white, brown, black. He finds a dirty pink blanket, a plastic milk crate, makes a bed. They've been alone all night. No protection, no food. I was afraid they'd be dead. But when Michael comes toward me, I hear mewling. Eyes still closed—they're a couple of days old.

Sharon in the intake office opens her closet, comes out with a box of Similac in tiny bottles, nipples to attach to each. Michael sits down on a bench in the playground, reaches out his hands the way you'd cup water, takes a puppy from Sharon, yellow milk. So I sit beside him for puppy number two, white, one ear wet. He doesn't know how to suck yet. A girl opens the puppy's mouth for me so I can get the milk taste on his tongue. We don't have nine sets of hands, so the black puppy is still unfed. When I share the bottle with him, he sucks and sucks without a breath. I'd burp him, but he's drinking away, almost the entire bottle.

And then he falls asleep on my forearm, in the flower beads of my black sweater, his mouth open, pink tongue lolling. Dreaming. He shits on my arm, a glittery iridescent green that someone brushes away. Yesterday, I'd seen his mother—auburn, shag coat, at ease with her big belly in the parking lot so rank with piss. I blew each breath back out as if I were filling balloons. When I'd headed toward the shelter's main door, she'd gone toward the portable building. The president walks outside the main doors, sees me sitting with the clients and the puppies. Sees the bottle in my hand. Shakes his head.

I need to raise two and a half million dollars in grants a year, just for the basics. Every night, 750 people live here, eat here. Two hundred are children, most under seven years old.

In my dim office, I'm filling out government forms when the

CSI team drives up in their white truck. Cops block the side streets, round up the guys who fought in the overcrowded bathroom. One man stabbed another, though after the slew of cops arrives and they have the men in hand, the crime is downgraded to a slashing. Maybe the victim was high, someone says, and it didn't hurt so bad. I think one of them is the man who always waves to me in the morning, yelling, "Mami."

There is a new baby from the Salvation Army in the day care. The day care ladies busy with bottles and diapers, and Delia is crying on the carpet, so my arms are useful to pick her up. She settles in on my hip. Her eyelashes black, paintbrush wet, hair cloudy curls, almond eyes. Jowled cheeks of an old man. I hold Santa for her, and he said, *Hello*; Elmo said *Hello*, and a paper bird floating on a string, and finally Delia replies in song. It is like talking to a bird in my arms. I want to recline in the rocking chair with Delia, as I did the day my son was born, the only day the doctor let me rock him. When I give Delia to another woman and she cries, reaches for me from across the room, the woman laughs, said, "That's not your mother." But she won't be soothed, keeps reaching.

George knows me from day care, sees me coming in to work. Before I get to the front door, he leans against me, rests his face against my bare legs, the flowers on my skirt, as if I were a field. When I'd arrived at the shelter two years before, I wasn't even sure my body was still here.

The day Tiny turned three, she'd worn a blue bubble blouse, white striped with sleep. She saw the new lamplight coming from my office and walked inside. I heard her whisper to my desk: "Is there a present for me?" And I was ashamed of myself, but Tiny kept looking. She walked up to each lamp, saying, "I like your light." Her whole outfit was new: white barrettes, a purple satin purse that Iris gave her. I was so grateful to Iris of the big eyes and dangly earrings that spelled her name. When Iris said, "You're beautiful," Tiny said, "My name is Tiny, not Beautiful." Tiny, Mary, Kadesha each high-five, screech from the jungle gym on seeing me—yelling, "My friend"—each kiss blown, wave, and touch is a light. Here, my knees are coming back where a child hung on.

Australia

First, there's the squall of walking down the narrow aisle with my too-big suitcase, navigating the bored stares of the already seated. The mutiny of belting in. Breath to my right, sneakers beside my feet, a boy turning a tight left to say, "Hi." Outstretched hand. His throat level with my eyes.

I'd already been building a transparent wall between seats, deeding him the armrest to avoid possible contact and conversation on the flight. But I look up. An open smile. Clear-eyed. A boy in his early twenties. My hand feels stationary, but I lift it from my silver buckle. My body already silting into the blue seat, but I lean forward, give him my hand. "I'm going to Boston to visit my dad's relatives," the boy says. He's been traveling many hours, from Australia. "I haven't seen them since I was eight."

"Did you like them?" I wonder if it was like my visits to cousins I saw once a year, standing in their grass, sitting at their table, admiring them from an aquatic distance. The boy says that it's hard to remember. But there's something low, fine cinders—some nerves, I guess.

The boy's hair is black, which doesn't address the issue of darkness. The voice of the flight attendant is essentially a tube color, midrange cad red, permanent green. But her demonstration is acid yellow, and it's hard to follow her instructions, meet her bright eyes. I'll have to locate the exit doors later.

On the adjoining seat rest, I forget and touch the boy's arm, the basilic vein running up the inside. Really it was both our arms, the accidental touching of elbows, forearms. The boy is a little younger than my son would be. I imagine my son would be like this, saying hello, giving his hand to a stranger traveling alone. The contact is a little trance. "I work in a library," he says. Points to his dad a few seats ahead, on the aisle. That helps explain his reading a little, the *Wind-up Bird Chronicle* in his bag, his love of Anne Michaels's *Fugitive Pieces,* which I share. Which I've never shared with anyone sitting next to me. All his book talk. It's like a steady combing of my hair.

There are sound worlds we can't hear unless someone brings them into our register. After we've talked for a long time, the boy says, "I'm going to sleep for a little while, but I'll be back." It is so considerate—to tell me that he's going to close his eyes, so that I don't feel shut out. A little kindness. He listens to music—I can hear it, faraway voices. When his leg leans against mine in sleep, I'm asleep. If you live a life with another or many, maybe it's nothing, maybe you wouldn't even notice it. Like the leaning of a suitcase. The closest I can get to my son's body is to touch the grass over his grave. When I wake up, the boy's leg resting against mine brushes away years of dirt. Like a spell.

I remember the monastery near Dublin where the monks couldn't talk all day, except while walking in a short corridor—having to say everything in those moments. And the castle in Killarney where the rich people who'd once owned the place slept sitting up in bed in case of fire, the guide said, so that smoke would have to rise higher to kill them. The boy and I slept like them. It was just a flight, city to city, but I don't know how it's done, how we're carried in the sky, set down somewhere else.

At the end of the trip, I stand up fast in the aisle while the boy is still sitting, fit myself in the aisle between the others. But I hand him a book with poems for my son. He unzips his bag, packs the book, zips it back, all the while looking at my face. Something has shifted, and he looks surprised. He talks, but his voice sounds underwater. In baggage claim in Boston, I see the boy standing with his father, the father staring at me as if he would like to speak. His mouth is open.

I like to think of the book traveling with the boy, home to Australia, my voice on the other side of the world. I had a teacher who fell in love with an Australian playwright. The playwright wrote a radio drama called *I Walked into My Mother*. She sent me the tape. Aboriginal children were taken from their parents and given to white people to be raised. So the children didn't even know their parents. One of the children walked into his mother without knowing her. As if a mother is a door.

There is something I meant to say to the boy. It has to do with the Navy's alcohol treatment center that I attended after I gave my son away. The sailors had to do psychodramas in the cafeteria. There was a little dais, like a raised white starfish, but flat enough for chairs. "You don't have to do it," my counselor had said. As if my drinking was less serious since I was so young, my job not on the line. I was relieved. I watched one sailor stand on the starfish as himself, with another sailor who took on the role of his dad. What was surprising is how quickly the sailor saw his dad in the other sailor. His voice heated. How when the other sailor spoke, the son heard his father. There was yelling—the son had questions to ask. I wondered how the dad sailor answered him, standing so close, unprotected. The son still stranded, but when the other sailor reached out to him, you could see it was the father who held him. Sometimes when I see a boy who could be my son's age, if he'd lived, I think about reincarnation again. I think, it could be him. But with the boy from Australia it's something else too. When he spoke to me, leaned so close, I was still stranded, but could feel something of who my son might have been. Kind, relaxed, a reader. I didn't know how to talk to the boy when we're back on the ground—I rush past him, as if I have somewhere to go. Worried I'll make a misstep, and the boy or the father will think I've attached too much importance to a conversation in flight.

Informant

The night my son died, someone must have called the house. Did I hear the phone ring? It was May 27, 1982. I had turned twenty-one just a few days earlier. He died at 5:30 p.m. I was likely in the shower then, washing my hair. Getting ready to go over to Sophie's. From my closet, I take a silver dress. Carry it to the living room, the break behind the easy chairs and breakfast table. Unfold the ironing board. My dad is in one of the chairs, facing the TV. When I iron, silver metal on my silver dress, no one yells. Even though it's clear I'm going out. No one threatens me, reminds me of my curfew. My dad's face is soft when he watches me talking while I iron out the wrinkles. He's holding on to what I don't know, so I can live in the world not knowing for a while. "I hope you have a good time," he says. My parents never say that to me anymore. I'm nervous, chattering about the beach, my friend from work, her boyfriend's band that we're going to go hear on the pier. I'm afraid someone will stop me, and I need to go out. My dad is speaking to me kindly, as if I am another daughter. Someone who can be trusted.

My son's burial was June 2. No one told me. It's on the death certificate. There is a box that says, "Type of Disposition." Underneath, someone wrote in block letters: "BURIAL." The next box says, "Date of Disposition." The date is written here. There is another box that says, "Informant—Name and Address." My uncle's name is here. In the Relationship box is written "Father."

With a stick of chalk, I draw a circle around you. When water is taken away, drink from the cup of my hands. When my hands are cut off, eat from my mouth. Remember, go only as far as the sky is blue.

May 27 was a Friday, and that Friday night a girl I worked with at the train car restaurant got her boyfriend Al to put me and Sophie on a guest list. An earlier night, when the girl and I had been working the hostess stand, she'd told me she'd been raped when she was younger. There were no customers just then. In the dim light of the service bar, she stood close to the wall. It seemed like the wall of her house, the window a man had climbed in. She's a small girl, black hair to her waist, straight-backed like a chair. She spoke with no embarrassment, no shame. "I pressed charges," she said. "He went to jail." We wore matching outfits, black Danskin leotards and skirts, ballet slippers. As if we were going to class. I couldn't imagine how she had survived that, thought it would just carve a person out. I couldn't ask her any questions. Just listened, and then it felt weird to stop listening, greet customers. Ask, "How many for dinner?"

Sophie and I drive to Daytona, an hour's drive. At the pier, two bands share a tiny dressing room. It's empty at first, just us, the girl, and Al. The girl applying shiny blue eyeshadow up high on her eyelids. She says, "I'm sorry about Dave hitting on you. It really makes me mad that he'd try to pick you up, knowing you're a friend of mine." She looks like a tiny princess in her cloak of dark hair fringed at the ends, cobalt glitter, regal bearing. We'd passed the rest of the band in the bar on our way backstage.

"Oh, it didn't really bother me," I said.

"He's just about engaged," the girl said.

"Oh." I envy how the girl seems to live in a world where people behave. How she has standards for behavior and gets offended when they're broken.

"No," Al said. "He and Sheila broke up again last week." The door opens, and the band files in. Dave squeezes between me and Sophie on the couch. I try to wriggle my arm out from under his.

He smiles. "What's the matter? You aren't afraid of me."

I try to look bored. "No."

"Good. I'm glad to hear that." He hands me a quart bottle of Jim Beam. "Here." I wish he wouldn't look so amused, smirky. He twirls a piece of my hair. I show off, chug several swallows straight from the bottle. Hand it back. He laughs. The club's manager opens the dressing room door and peers in. He wears flared polyester pants and a pale green T-shirt with the band's logo on it. Thick dark hair falls to his shoulders in carefully hairsprayed layers. "Watch that guy," Dave whispers. "When he looks at something, he moves his entire upper body in that direction. He never moves just his head 'cause he's afraid of messing up his hair."

The next morning, I come to, with Dave, in a quiet house in what looks like countryside. His house, I guess. I remember a white closet. I see the tiny white swans on my hips, scars from when I was pregnant with Tommy. Windows, and outside fields and fields. It's nothing like Orlando or Daytona. As if we've crossed state lines or gone to another country. I've never seen a place like this. A house in the center of grass, no others in sight.

I don't call home. No one knows where I am. After two days, I come back. I don't remember how. No one is home at my parents' house. It's so quiet. Air-conditioner hum. Go in my bedroom to change clothes, gather a few things up to take with me, in case there's yelling. My gold carpet is strewn with thick pieces of pink plastic, like fingers and toes. My mom had bought thick, solid plastic shoe racks for me to match my pink canopy. The night my son died and I disappeared, she'd gone in my room. Taken each shoe rack and ripped them to pieces. But the shoe racks weren't rippable—even scissors wouldn't cut through. Maybe a big knife, but it would be hard work. I don't know how she did it with her bare hands. I don't know my son has died. I'm terrified she can be so mad at me.

One minute I'm alone, the next my parents appear. Not mad. I can't figure it out—I'd been gone for days, I hadn't called, the destroyed shoe racks. My dad said, "Tommy died. Friday night." I don't remember screaming. We're standing by the long kitchen counter, by the phone. My dad puts the phone book in my hands, says, "Tear it," when he sees my hands are tearing at the air. He said, "Your mother did it with the shoe racks."

Mark and Julia come back to our house in Orlando after my son dies. They quit their jobs, buy a travel trailer, and drive around the country. One day, they just show up our door. Spend the night. In the morning, they're leaving secretly. I'm still in my pajamas, but I hear them. I catch them by the side door to the garage. The way they'd left with Tommy. "Didn't you want to say good-bye to me?" I ask. Mark and Julia both said words I don't remember. Nothing about my son. Mark leans his head down a little, as if giving in to something. It must be nice to be two people, to always have someone else there who can talk if you can't. Mostly, we just look at each other. No one says anything to me about Tommy. Nothing at all.

Years later, I meet a woman in a writing workshop whose adopted brother had died in a car accident. She wrote that her father thought about the birth mother all the time. And the woman said, "Dad. All the time?" And he said, "Yes." He thought about the mother showing up at his house and asking about her son. He thought about what could he say to her. Our teacher at the workshop had been concerned for the father. He said, "ALL the time? Why doesn't she try to get him some help?" But I was thrilled. The birth mother wasn't invisible. She wasn't a receptacle. I thought if this mother can matter so much, maybe I can matter. Maybe my aunt and uncle think about what they will say to me when I show up at their door.

Guanyin

1.

Before I see her, I drive from the beach to Orlando. I take a plane to Boston, I'm on a bus to the Cape. At 4 p.m., it's dark out. An hour later, it could be midnight. It's Thanksgiving 2009, and I'm going to my aunt and uncle's house in Falmouth. On the bus, my heartbeat is so frantic, I wonder if I could have a heart attack.

Pale blue water tower—Brockton houses through trees. On the bus, the window is split with a silver bar, and I keep looking from one to the other, trying to see through the trees—*you're in there, you're in there. Infant* from Latin *infans*, unable to speak. The cold that comes through the glass is calming. An almost extinct language was spoken here. The bones in my face lean into it. Then it's Rockland, then Mansfield, over the bridge—the bridge! The lights on aisles of water. The water coming toward us, and the bridge carries us, holds us. I have a postcard of Abraham being promised a son, three angels—all of it surrounded by broken red glass. The wings of the angels feathery like birds. Everyone seems to float above the ground. Over the bridge I can breathe more easily—this is near home, though still only the Upper Cape, still strange. The first town on this side is Bourne. A man on the bus says, "Twenty years ago, this was all dark road."

I was here one other time, when I was seventeen years old. Holly, my friend from Bridgewater State College—Nicole's roommate—stayed at the Falmouth Campground in the summer, in a trailer with her mother. A group of kids, families, came every year. She'd invited me to visit. I'd arrived at the campground before Holly, before my boyfriend, Burgess, the one who'd been acquired by proximity—her boyfriend's best friend. I waited at a picnic table, ignored in a whispery way by dozens of kids my age, a little older. The kind of crowd that could populate "The Lottery"—a sunny day, I could imagine them lazily reaching into the green grass for rocks to stone me. Then one of Holly's friends, Tommy, came over. The first boy I'd met whose attention wasn't also a loneliness, no river between. He sat down at the table with me, spoke with ease and kindness. Normalcy. His hair curled like mine, but black, soft as eyelashes.

Tommy left for Martha's Vineyard that afternoon, while I was deep in the woods with Burgess, his party late into the night. Around my neck I wore the opal Burgess gave me, swam to him in the dark lake, barely able to see him. But when Burgess went into town for more beer with his friends who were still ignoring me as if they were the original Pilgrims, then I heard the boys were back from the island. When Tommy appeared, he and I somehow separated from everyone else. The ground like an escalator down the sand path in the woods. His words inside, disappearing where trees finally met. I wanted to stay with him. But Burgess drove up in his Jeep with the unfriendly friends, said, "Get in if you're coming." Tommy lived in a tent with his sister and mom, where would I sleep? Sand in the wet cuffs of my jeans. I took my seat in the Jeep though Burgess would desert me that summer at a concert in Hyannis, and Holly would say, "You have to fight for him." But he looked bleary kissing one of the Pilgrim girls. And when we were together, daylight was too realistic, like Finland, a constant documentary—

the woods always seemed on the precipice of murder, the ocean I loved went wan and scrawny. We were only good in silence at night: Clapton, drinking, and sex. A sunny-looking guy, but it didn't shine on me. I wish I had been the girl who waved, said *I'll get a ride*, the girl who walked into the trees.

At my aunt and uncle's house, there is a crowd in the kitchen: my uncle's aunt Ellen, my aunt's sisters, Cliff their neighbor, whom I met for a moment two years ago in his salmon shirt. Many others. Six dogs. I'm on the outskirts again—they don't know me, don't know why I'm here. Hours ago they finished their holiday dinner, but they've stayed to say hello to me. "She was a little girl the last time you saw her," Julia tells her sisters, who seem like twins in height, expression. One says, "Oh, you have a friend in Newton." As if this is the purpose of my visit. At sixty, Julia is still so pretty—her face delicate and fine. A girl's face. A heroine's.

Technically, their house is not a mansion, but it feels like one. The many rooms and multiple staircases, fireplaces. With the crowd, it could be the setting for a Chekhov play. Chekhov, who in his glasses actually looks like Eric Clapton. The relatives and guests leave quickly. "It's not you," several women say, like echoes, laughing. Julia makes me a plate. I feel like a beggar. The dogs at my feet on the metal rung of the bar stool. Detached from the floor, my body could float, be upside-down. *Sorry*, I'd say. *Sorry*.

The walls feel like plates, crackable. I'm not hungry, but I chew. My aunt and uncle sit on either side of me. A fire is lit between two walls. "Is everything okay with you and your dad?" one of them asks me. I'd been afraid to phone Mark and Julia to say I was coming. But two weeks before, I'd been visiting my parents. My mother mentioned that Julia had emailed my dad. I went on his computer, found her address. Brought it home. When I emailed Julia to say I'd be in Boston over Thanksgiving, that I'd like to stop by, I said I didn't want to mention the trip to my parents. Said I didn't want to hurt their feelings as I wasn't spending the holiday with them.

But they're confused. I can see they're wondering why would I come here and keep it a secret from my parents, ask them not to mention it? They are uneasy, our conversation triple-spaced. Leaning into the island, faces turned toward me, elbows on granite—we make a tableau. She's lily-like. His eyes are magnified, underwater. Oh, I am a wrong number. Even making conversation with cashiers in the grocery store exhausts me, and I'm here with almost no notice, sitting in a kitchen with people who barely know me. Here for days and days. Everything feels off. A child would be welcome here—a child would fit in. But I am too old for this house; I know why people choose the endless time after death, that quiet, but it's always terrible when someone stops singing. The three of us create some kind of hum. Invisible bees circle us, raising the hair on my arms. I've changed my mind. I want to retract everything, reverse my trip, go back over the bridge, get back to my quiet duplex with the ocean outside. Nobody asking me questions. Mark says, "Why don't you call your father and wish him a Happy Thanksgiving?"

I say no, and then I say, "Okay," and Mark dials on his cell.

He's bowled over—that's what my dad says to Julia when I give her the phone. He can't imagine why I'm here.

It's sickening—hurting him. I have to call him back. Mark gives me his phone, which I take, though I have my own phone in my purse. I leave them, go up the stairs, down the long hall past the many bedrooms, to the peach room. I don't want to hurt my mom either. My dad says that he thinks he has it figured out, thinks I'm here to meet a guy from an online dating service who lives in this town. I'd mentioned him to them last summer, as something light—a funny story—looking for someone to date on the internet. But they'd worried it to pieces—how could I date someone so far away? I hadn't even met the guy in person—he'd been too busy, he said.

After talking to them, I can't sleep, worrying about having hurt them. Then I sleep, but not before my heart is panicking as it did on the plane, on the bus. I'm so sorry I've come here. I forget why I've come, what our connection is.

But then it's light. Julia greets me good morning in the kitchen and kisses my cheek. I think a little later, "She remembers." There aren't any birds in the trees here—a leaf swaying in the wind I mistook for a bird, familiar movement in trees. It's cold here, but something blue is blooming outside.

A bird flew beside the window and up, rising as it approached me. Gray-blue feathers above, white below, headed up high. There's a stone wall outside—a boulder wall and brown-red leaves piled behind it. A wall someone built to contain what they want to keep.

Tell me what you remember—from the moment you got in the car in the garage in Orlando and drove away. He was crying, the last I heard him then, going into the garage or in the car. Tell me everything you remember from then on. How was the plane ride? Did he mind it? Did he sleep? I practice my questions for Julia, sitting alone at a little table upstairs in a big room with a fireplace, a sound system. Mark had asked me, "What kind of music do you like?" I didn't know how to describe what I like. I choose one genre called "Acoustic," blue or another color, and a Scottish singer I like started singing. It's really two rooms, two sets of couches— a movie-screen against the far facing wall, the door in around the corner. An inset white beam near the sound system monitor blocks my view of the door, secludes me beyond the fireplace.

On the tallest trees, the tops are bare of leaves. Partway down the trees, some branches go straight out instead of up. Here they don't seem to be raised in escape, more like they are reaching to touch. The trees at peace. It'll be white. It'll be snow. All this low green buried. The yellow leaves like playing card spades. Thin stalked plant with small red hearts and tongues limp, something torn out. Another made of green-yellow stars. One with diamond leaves, red and yellow, that hang heavy though they must be thin as silk—drop earrings—white flowers at the top and on the ground. All of it lifting up the cloudy sky.

Julia said, "If you want to go into town, you can drive the Jeep." Town sounds like one big whiteness, like being hit in the face and then trying to find the right road. What would I do in town? I remember the bus station, the ride in the car with Mark, arriving at this dead-end road. Years ago, I saw a restaurant on the water, but I'm not sure it was Falmouth. Can I drive to Brockton, to the cemetery? Can I ask that? It's not around town—maybe that's what she means, that's it's only okay for a short distance. And can I ask that and not be hurtful? On a highway alone, I could calm down, rely on strangers. Today is Friday. There's still Saturday. There's Sunday. When can I ask about Tommy? On Sunday maybe, the day before I leave? So it's not so hard afterward? The snow will be on all of it. I can see flames in the window, small, falling and rising up over the peaceful trees which live just the same.

2.

This house is brand new. There won't be any baby clothes here, no baby shoes. "Sorg" was the first English word for sorrow, distress; "sorgian" is grieve. The wind is "windan"—move fast, circle round, twist, wave. "Wunden" is twisted as of ornamentation. Can be confused with "wund": injury, wound. When words were made, someone needed these. It's Friday night, and no one in this house has said his name. We rode in a silver car in the dark, on the southwestern tip of Cape Cod, glacier beneath us. Yards of water between us and the Elizabeth Islands, tiny islands owned by the rich, a family apiece. Three miles north over the water is Martha's Vineyard—the ferry leaves from here. If you miss the last one, there's nothing until morning. Boston is seventy miles south. Julia had asked me if I liked "bar pizza." I've never had pizza in a bar, but I can tell she thinks it's special. So I said yes, I'd like to try that. The day after Thanksgiving, they think the pizza place will be slow, but the parking lot is almost full. "It's one of the busiest days of the year," the hostess says. Between the cashier counter and the booths, the waitresses run. The three of us stand by a circle of wood, like a tree, waiting a long time for a table. I'm always in the way of one waitress, her tray of plastic glasses, and Mark puts his arm around my shoulders, pulls me in to stand closer to them. But I inch backward, annoy the waitress, come toward Mark and Julia again. I know I have my son's face, his eyes looking into their faces. Anxiety is a brocade, webbed inside—standing so close to my aunt and uncle is like trying to breathe through heavy fabric. My eyes could be rhinestone ornaments. I was at their wedding in 1969, seven or eight years old—ankleted, buttoned, laced, slippered, with their beauty above me. The wedding was a kingdom—the King and Queen live there—I pointed it out to my brother, a year younger. Pointing out the colors, the spires. That was back when I could tell him to pack his belongings into a paper shopping bag, hide it under his bed until morning, until he put on his Superman outfit, grabbed the bag, followed me out the door in my sunsuit and sandals, walking beside me down the street, clothes spilling out behind us. Trusting I knew where to go.

Finally seated, my aunt and uncle are across from me in the booth. It feels a little like a job interview. I could be made of felt, cut into the shape of a woman—I keep arranging an expression on my face that is the opposite of crying. The opposite of something is cutting into me. Earlier that day, we'd driven to Wood's Hole, and I stood in the rain taking pictures of water. Julia had said, "We could go to the aquarium." Boxes of water, a blue lobster. Two harbor seals that made a regular circuit in their pool, bobbing up like mermaids. Mark had said, "Look at his eyes." One seal had dark eyes, but the other's were almost colorless, the blue-gray of the seal's body, water. He was blinded from a shark attack—by the punctures or the trauma, they don't know which. Someone found him on a beach. Mark sees what I don't—the blindness, the tanks of fish that live between two walls like the fire in his house. He hadn't wanted to come here. "There's no parking," he'd said. But then he found a spot.

I'd seen another harbor seal in Wellfleet a few years ago, after dinner at my parents' house. Cloudy, Mayo Beach had been almost deserted. Down a stretch between the rocks, over another set of rocks, were four people: one man taking a sailboat out just to anchor it, a woman standing at the edge of the shore, another man farther down the beach near more rocks—he had a scoop net in his hands, and a small boy played with him in the shallowest water. It was so quiet, but the tide wasn't all the way up, and I'd been glad there was room to walk. In the quiet gray sky and water, I'd walked up to a creature. At first, I didn't know what I was seeing. A baby seal with eyes like dark pools, lashed like a kitten, whiskered like one too. And like a baby, when I talked to him/her, the baby yawned. Flippered feet tucked together in back, toward the water. Smaller flippers on either side were tucked under too, like a folded letter. There was no alarm from the seal, but I didn't know what to do. She was completely out of the water, and I thought, I'll need to pick her up, help her back into the harbor. It will be like touching a fish, I thought, but different—skin like a wetsuit. I wondered if the seal had teething teeth like a child, wondered how a seal eats fish—if she'll bite.

I waved to the boat man—no response. I started to wave to the woman, but she jumped into the sea. I didn't want to leave the seal, but I needed help, so walked fast to the faraway net man with the boy. He said, "The seal was sunbathing two and half hours ago. Someone called Audubon. They said she's not hurt, it's natural. Just stay a hundred fifty feet away from her." The net man said, "That's why there's a sign." But there was no sign. I estimated 150 feet from the seal, sat on the rocks where I could see her. All the people on the beach went away, the tide came in far enough to wet her tail, and she turned on her side in the water. Sometimes she lifted her head and tail in an S-like yoga pose. When the water was high, she swam in that same position. For a long time, I saw her nose sticking up out of the harbor, in different places. She liked the blue raft anchored near shore, as if it was a creature too. Then she moved out past it. I was so glad to have looked into her eyes, spoken to her. I'm surprised when an animal doesn't talk back, and it's just trancing beauty. A few times, when she swam, I saw the folds of her coat beneath the waves.

The next day, I'd thought about going to the harbor, to just look for the seal. But what was I looking for? Wouldn't she be gone if all was well? I went to the library, and it was late afternoon, early evening when I got to the beach. A white van in the harbor circle parking lot: Marine Mammal Rescue. Were the Audubon people here to check on the seal? Was she still here? A man and woman came up from the beach. The woman had a shovel with a bright yellow handle. The man had a plastic bag with something dark in it. I said, "You're not here for the seal?"

The woman said, "Yes. He didn't make it." We're calling the seal "he."

"He died?"

"Yes," she says something euphemistic like "passing." She's young. The man doesn't want to meet my eyes—he just carries the bag, keeps walking toward the back door of the van.

"But, yesterday, they said she wasn't sick." I am too upset to know what pronoun is right to use.

"She was thin, and she had wounds." I remember little holes like pennies near her head. "We took samples to find out more." Shouldn't a rescue truck be able to rescue? Try to rescue? Why had they left her thin and wounded? She had opened her mouth for me in that sweet yawn. Couldn't they have just dropped a fish in there? Helped her? I'm sorry I left her side. Later, I read that the rescuers like to leave baby seals in the water, in hopes that the mother is coming back. The next day I swam in the harbor where she swam, right by her rocks. Her grave out there somewhere.

At the Wood's Hole Aquarium, the other seal had been stranded at a month old, unable to feed itself, wounded too. They brought her here. I take pictures of her swimming. Mark and Julia and I make a little group, looking at the same fins, bones. Sea stars that will appear again the next day when we walk on Plymouth Beach with the dogs. Julia will say, "You don't see them anymore." But every few steps, there will be another between the rocks, on the sand. Starfish like hands outstretched. I take a picture of Mark and Julia looking at me in the rain.

In the booth at the pizza place, Julia is excited to go home and watch a movie on the big screen upstairs—a comedy. It sounds fun. But once we get in the room, in our chairs, she suggests a movie about a child raised by someone not his mother. It's no comedy, and I panic, say, "No." So, Mark scrolls through more movie choices—he'll buy the one we choose. We all want something funny, but there is only one. A boys' movie that turns out to be one obscenity after another. Louder on the big screen. It is like being bludgeoned. "Is it okay?" Mark asks. I know they're embarrassed; I'm embarrassed. We're trapped in this awkward room. We watch the main character, a famous comedian, have sex with one girl, then another. James Taylor appears at one point, asks the comedian if he ever gets tired of talking about his dick. We can't even manage to pick a movie, how can we ever talk about my son? Finally Julia walks out. So, soon after, I do too.

3.

In the morning, when I come down the stairs, the six dogs bark their heads off as if I'm an intruder. Which I am. My aunt and uncle are early risers; I'm late. But they wait to eat breakfast with me at the island in the center of the kitchen, the dogs gone back to sleep in their individual beds arrayed under the big windows. Two dogs sleep next to each other like twins. I'm slow drinking my coffee, and Mark goes upstairs to his office. Julia is on a chair beside me. I ask her fast, I've practiced—"Can I talk to you about Tommy?" I know she knows all the words I've said, that she's heard me, but there's a white space. She says she remembers my asking about him last time, my wanting to talk two years ago. "It's why I'm here," I tell her.

One of the dogs is seventeen years old, blind and deaf, covered in long hair—her whole world dark and ending. When she bumps her head into a corner of the kitchen, Julia turns the dog's body to face another direction. A big dog bumps against me until I pet him.

Julia and I talk over the sink. "I don't know how you did it," she says, meaning how I gave him to her. "I was prepared," she said. She had thought I might change my mind. Julia said she came to me in the hospital, stood next to my bed and said, "He'll always know who his birth mother is." She said I said, "Not until he's eighteen." And she was surprised. I'm surprised. Why would I have said such a thing? It sounds as though I'm parroting. Like the story of my dad not knowing his father wasn't his biological father until he was eighteen. She said it was never a secret where Tommy came from, who his mother was, not to her family. Maybe Mark's—she looks unsure about that. Wouldn't she know that? I think that means Mark's family didn't know—it was a secret. Why? And why does her face keep changing, as if she's remembering something, but uncertain how to say it? Tommy's related by blood to Mark's family. Why wouldn't they want to know that? I try to see myself in that hospital bed, Julia standing beside me, but it's like a movie I glimpsed once, changing channels.

"We never knew who Tommy's father was, or anything about your situation," Julia said. I tell her that I'd been engaged before I got pregnant, but fell out of love. That when I'd tried to break up with my fiancé, he'd said, "You're not trying hard enough." I didn't tell her that when I told my ex-fiancé I was pregnant, he tried to convince me to have an abortion, and I wouldn't. I told her that my ex's family wanted to adopt my baby, that his mother phoned me and asked, "When will we get our bundle of joy?" I didn't tell her that he'd stalk me at work and school, follow me to my car. But when I said that I'd finally told him the baby wasn't his, my aunt smiles like a mother. She smiles in admiration and a kind of surprised pride. "I was ready to go to court and say it," I tell her. "I didn't know about DNA." My aunt said, "They didn't really have the test then."

Julia said that Tommy had an earache before Christmas—December 9 or 19. That was when it started. The doctors kept thinking it was a virus. But he didn't feel good at Christmas, and by New Year's Eve they knew it was leukemia. She said that they have a beautiful tree in the basement, but that my uncle still doesn't like to put it up, because Christmas is when Tommy got sick. She said he still won't talk about Tommy. My son is as present in their lives as he is in mine. That sorrow wasn't short-term for anyone. It changed us the way cancer changed my son's DNA.

While we talk, sometimes I still feel as though my face is a mask. But then my aunt says that the next step in my son's treatment was going to be a bone marrow transplant. That he needed to get a little better first. She tells me, "That's when you were going to get the call. You were going to be his donor." Then I cried. I had what he needed. I could have given it to him, helped him, my body could have saved him. But he couldn't get strong enough for the transplant.

Someone's in the room next door—it's Mark. He'd come down the other stairway, been right beside us, unheard. "Did you just come downstairs?" my aunt asks.

"I've been here the whole time," he says. I don't know what to say.

"I guess I'll go upstairs," I say to them.

At the round table I'm just looking out the window. Then someone is rushing through the doorway I can't see, running toward me. It's Mark—I know he's not laughing, but what is he doing? His body looks destabilized, seismic. He's convulsing like someone being punched in the chest, hunched forward. I try to see his face in the reverberations, but he's moving so quickly toward me. I can see he's crying now, shaking. In his hands are envelopes, a giant photo, tapes.

His voice is so loud, as if his words are one on top of another—the same words said over and over. Mark's arms are around me before I can hear what he's saying. No one has ever held me so tightly. It's a shock to matter this much. It isn't like arms are around me, it's more like a house, as if he has made a house around me. As he did around Tommy. As I did in Florida when Tommy was sick and I couldn't go to him, when he was dying, when he died, I made my arms a cradle. When I'd go to sleep at night, I arranged my arms and hands into a bed for him.

Mark says, "I just loved him so much." It takes a long time to say. I could engrave it, I could carve it in the air. The things in his hands have been dropped on the table. His arms are still so hard they feel permanent, that even when he lets go, I'll feel them. I understand that he is holding me and Tommy too. I'm afraid of this much sadness. It's not kept in a room of his body, it's his whole body grieving. Maybe he knew what he was doing, keeping it under wraps—who am I to ask him to talk? I hadn't understood what it had been like for him, for Julia, to hold my son, their son, day after day, touch and hear, to love him in person. And to feel him become thin, sick, see the lost look. It could not have been easy for them to face me. What is it like to lose someone and see them looking back at you in someone else's face?

My own grief seems to go down deep in the guilt of hurting Mark. Julia will tell me that Mark could do this for me because he loves me. She didn't know about the drawer with Tommy's photos. She wondered if Mark would open the drawer when she was at work. Look at the photos by himself. I don't know who I am that I can be loved this much.

And a weird power comes back too, makes me feel I've manipulated Mark and Julia. There's a mad scientist moment of having them in a kind of thrall. But mostly I'm numb. Why is it such a shock to be loved? Why can I only feel it for a second—a warmth in my chest—before I detach?

Julia said that when we'd been discovered in the kitchen, Mark had said to her, "That was a long talk you were having."

And Julia had said, "Kelle wants to know about Tommy." She said that's when he went to the drawer. Took all the things out and started to hand them to her, saying, "Give these to Kelle." Then he said, "No, I'll do it." And he'd come rushing up the stairs. All of it inside, all these years. And now he's talking about Tommy because I asked him to, because he loves me. I'm still numb, but it feels as though I'm materializing, like a time traveler. My atoms knitting together in one place.

Before this day, the only pictures I'd seen of my son were in the hospital when he was born, his first few days, and before he died. Only a couple of times in between. But in these envelopes, I find him. Here he is—happy, happy boy smiling at me. Mark holds Tommy to his chest at the beach, the trunk of the car open behind them. In the sun, my son rests against my uncle's chest. Mark's hair is long, he's fit, tan; Tommy is baby chubby, and they lean into each other so contented, relaxed, father and son. Nothing bad has touched them; no inkling of harm. It's all one happiness. Standing beside me now, the color has gone from my uncle's hair, lines run like scratches across his cheeks.

I'd thought my son lived in the past in their lives, that now they had the dog hotel, the new house, their friends with whom they went to Ireland, golf and gardening and things from this century. I thought I was alone with the whole of it, my son's photo sleeping in the house with me. Julia comes up the stairs, into the room. She hands me a gold locket, with Tommy's picture in it. I feel faraway. Her eyes are very open. It's her locket—I can't understand this yet. It's jewelry, it's a tiny photo of Tommy that they'd sent to me and my parents at Christmas. He's in a swing, wearing a sweater that makes him look very strong, like a football player.

"What about the hope chest?" Mark asks. "With Tommy's things?" It's in Mansfield. "It's only forty-five minutes, I'll go." And he's gone.

4.

It's almost Christmas, 1981. My son, their son, is standing in front of Mark, who holds a stocking that is almost as tall as Tommy. At the top is part of an *O*, an *M*. A snowman smiles midway down. Tommy's smiling, one hand by his hip, one arm lifted, bent at the elbow. I can count his fingers. He's wearing green corduroy overalls, a long-sleeved white shirt with red and green, white baby shoes. I can only smile when I look at him—he is so happy. Bright eyes.

Tommy is on a horse, holding the wooden handles above the horse's head. He has a dark jacket on over red pants like pajamas, a butterfly shape at one knee, green socks. Someone is holding him steady. Children play in the wallpaper behind him. His face is serious, looking at the photographer. It is my face too. I am looking into my eyes, his eyes. If this is Christmas, he is already sick.

Another smiling photo—the warm red pants, white socks with his feet turned out, a white shirt with red stripes, and the word COWBOY in navy repeated over and over. A gigantic stuffed dog three times his size is just behind him. He's looking up with his bright eyes again, smiling.

In his playpen, four fingers in his smiling mouth, his other hand in motion as if he's about to wave. His fingers long like mine. Strawberry blond hair curling. Red shirt, blue. Bunny lying down. One finger pointing. He looks as though he's having fun. Laughing.

Sitting on the back of a giant real dog, both of them on a couch. Tommy reaching one hand out to touch the dog's neck, one leg over the front of the resting dog. Wearing his cowboy shirt with the green overalls.

Earlier, October, 1981. He's seven months old. Sitting on my uncle's lap. Mark has his arms around Tommy, who has one leg outstretched on Mark's thigh, one falling between. In his hands, my uncle holds a small pumpkin, carved with a smile. Tommy holds the top of the pumpkin. One palm is outstretched near one of the pumpkin's eyes as if petting it. He's in light blue pajamas with feet. Beautiful. Julia told me about a psychic she listens to, reads. All this time, I thought she'd been gardening. I know what she's doing now, looking for a door.

Tommy's drinking from a bottle, sitting in a high chair with a yellow tray. Eyes happy, smiling. Now he's riding a Snoopy dog. Holding on to the train conductor's hat, feet on the carpet. His eyes so dark blue, flushed. Here Tommy looks like no one but himself, so beautiful I stop breathing. He looks lost. I would take off my body for him right now. Detach my bones, hand them over. He's not feeling well here, an indention near his eye, at his temple. There's confusion, sadness. He just got here, and now he's already going.

Tommy never learned to talk—never said any actual words. Julia said, "When he would have been learning, developing, he was fighting to live." There is a birthday photo I don't recognize, because he is tiny, thin, blond hair gone. He looks older and smaller at the same time, hand lifted to his chest, fingers in, smiling with his mouth closed, other hand reaching again. Julia has him in her arms, big smile, hand on Mark's hand. Tommy has an aqua blanket on his knees. My grandmother is smiling, sitting next to them. He's one year old. Almost gone. His eyes are very very blue.

There is a yellow balloon above Mark's head that says, "Happy Birthday Tom." "Did you call him Tom?" I ask.

"Yes," Julia says. "Tom-Tom." It's a shock to me, not knowing what name he was called. Tom.

Mark had come back with his arms full of bags. "I didn't open any of it—I just took it all." He placed it all on the dining room table. A speeding ticket in his hand. Just a warning. Julia with me at the table. Mark standing behind us. There is a clown at the party, cake, pointy hats. Tommy is sitting in Julia's lap smiling and laughing. I said, "He looks so happy even though he's sick."

"He was always like that," Julia said.

When she opens the Baby Book, Julia gasps. "There might not be much in here," she'd started to say, and then we see it is almost full. His first smile is two or two and a half months. His first laugh is four or four and a half months. His first incisor. "Which tooth is an incisor?" I ask.

"I don't know," Julia says, almost laughing. Because it was gone and now it's back—he's here, he's cutting a tooth. There's a favorite foods question, and one of the answers is "Beef."

And I say, "Beef?!"

And Mark or Julia says, "Yes, you know, in the little jars." It's a little funny because I'm a vegetarian, and they are slightly defensive about this. There's a medical history page. Julia points to "Dec 9" (or 19?) with the handwritten "earache." She says, "This is where it started." She says it was AML, acute myeloid leukemia, like the guy supposedly had in the awful movie we'd watched.

"Did it go into his spine?" I ask. Julia looks confused. "And then into his brain?" She doesn't know what I'm talking about. "Did he have a bump on his forehead? A tumor?"

"No," she said. "He had leukemia. There was nothing on his forehead. Look at the pictures—there's no bump." Where did I get this information? Why have I believed this for twenty-seven years? No spinal cancer, no brain cancer, no tumor on his forehead. She seems almost insulted that he could have had some kind of deformity, her boy.

After looking at his photos, when I look in the mirror, I see him in my face clearly. I see his mother. When we were going through the photos, I said, "He's so beautiful."

Julia said, "He looks like you." I couldn't say anything.

Mark gives me the five blue tapes, each about the size of the palm of my hand. White in the center, a hole in the middle of each. Tommy is on these tapes. He is alive on these tapes. I don't know how to play them. "Tommy 1st Birthday 1," and 2, 3, and 4. Another one is "Plymouth Beach 5 m and Tommy Smith & Mikie 8 m." He's inside these. Maybe even the sound of his voice, his laugh.

We're meeting my aunt's sister and her husband at an Irish pub. Julia and Mark like to go there and sing along. But the singer is late. Julia has driven us to the pub. Mark seems a little drunk, drinks a large beer there. I think I am to blame for this, I have opened this up. I ask Mark what he's going to have, and he says something like a T-bone, some kind of meat item. And then he says something to me, laughing a little, that I don't understand at first, can't respond to. But then I hear it, he said, "Beef, like Tommy." He's talking to me about Tommy, regardless of what it does to him.

I wind up insulting the husband of my aunt's sister. He wants to know if I like some writer of mysteries or thrillers, and I just say, "No," based on the name. I make a face. It's unkindly arrogant of me. The man says, "Are you a Democrat?"

I say, "Yes."

He says, "That explains it."

"I feel as though I've been pigeonholed," I say, laughing a little. Walking to the car, I say, "I hope I wasn't rude." I ask my aunt and uncle, "Are you Republicans?" It's 2009.

Julia says, "Yes."

Mark says, "Do you want to get in another car?" I laugh a little. Surprised.

Now that they know why I'm visiting them, there's no pretense of being there to write. I'm there to see them, so they stay with me all day. Julia gets a new cell phone at the store. We take two of the dogs to the beach in the Jeep, walk in the cold wind and sun. I had nothing warm enough for that—my one sweatshirt Florida-thin—so Julia gave me one of Mark's, fleecy inside, gray, with the name of a college that doesn't exist. A man played a bagpipe beside the ocean. The sun was setting fast over one of the bodies of water on either side of us—sound or bay, I don't know which—Mark driving with determination on the windy road, so we could get to see it over the water before it disappeared. Julia could see the red through the trees, "Look, look, it's falling." I looked, but Mark kept going, trying to get us to that beach. When we pulled into the parking lot, facing the ocean, there was a bright cap for a moment, then just the sea.

The last night, we pick up Mark's aunt Ellen and go to a nice restaurant for lobster. I'm worried I won't know how to eat it. So I copy what Ellen does. Julia had said she was unsure if Ellen knows I'm Tommy's mother. Ellen knew he was adopted. She's so close to Mark. Having saved him from the Brockton slum, transporting him to Boston to live with her, sending him to private school. But maybe they kept the part about me a secret.

Still, Julia said that Ellen lived in Boston when Tommy was sick, and she went to the hospital every single night. Can she see Tommy in my face? We don't mention him at dinner. But when we drop her off, Ellen blows me a kiss. At the homeless shelter, anytime I blew a kiss to a child in the hallway, she would hold her hand to her face, catch it. Always surprised. Like me.

In the morning, Julia goes to work, and Mark seems a little nervous to take me to the bus station. He says, "Do you have everything. Kleenex?" It's as if there's been some slippage of time—that he's forgotten I'm not eight or even eighteen. "I'm just trying to think of things your mother would want you to have." My mother. I know it's confusing—I'm confused too.

At the bus station, I've got the time wrong—I'm there far too early. "Do you want to come back home?" Mark asks. I don't want to bother him, don't know how to manage this good-bye. Home.

"No, I'll be fine—I'll stay here." He says something about calling him, and I misunderstand. I think he means I can call while I'm waiting for the bus. I say, laughing, "If I get bored?"

Mark says, "If you need anything." I don't mean to be off-hand, slighting him in any way. But it sort of feels that way, that

I could be misunderstood. I can't manage all the words. I don't know what to say. On the ride there, in the car, I'd turned toward him and said, "Thank you for being Tommy's parents." It was all I could do in the light of day, leaving. I'd told Julia too—when we'd first talked on Saturday morning. She'd asked if I regretted giving Tommy to them. "I can think of no better parents for him. You were perfect," I said. "I do wonder about the water though." The city, I meant.

5.

After that, I get on the bus to Boston, take a train to the museum. That's when I see her—Guanyin. The Bodhisattva of Compassion. She's been here in Boston since 1912, from China. I see her kind eyes, her three small discs like stone coins at her fingertips. She's smiling at me with her eyes sort of closed and open at the same time. I have an envelope in my purse with the pictures of my son that I'd never seen before—I'd taken twelve of them. I have the tapes of him at the beach, his first birthday in the hospital. "Tell them the tape is old," my uncle had said when he handed them to me. "The tape could be too brittle to handle," he'd said, his words made staccato by his crying. I think he'd opened one of the reels then, film the color of root beer, transparent. "You can have them put on a DVD. We tried, but we couldn't do it." He'd asked me to make a copy for them too. He mentioned the brittleness again, his crying like a gun that would quiet, go off. Surprising all of us. The pictures and tapes that had been in a secret drawer for twenty-seven years are in plastic bags in my purse.

I didn't know who the stone woman was, her hand lifted 1,429 years, since AD 580. I'm on my way to a stranger's house in a nearby city because I have no money for a hotel. I'll take another line of the train. But I've come to the museum first. For years, I've missed the haystack on fire that I'd seen here.

That time, I'd left my family on the Cape, rode the bus back and forth to Boston. It was ten, fifteen years ago. I'd happened on the room of haystacks then, the cool ones too, the cathedral and river. So surprised, I'd stopped. The light stunning me as if the painter had placed his hand on my face. I'd wept. And after seeing the paintings, on the bus ride back to the Cape, I'd wanted to get off in the dark in Brockton. Find my son's grave. But I'd just sat in my seat and been carried over the bridge.

Now it's been so many years since I've seen those paintings, I don't expect to see them again. It had just been a special show, I thought. On this visit to the museum, I get lost immediately. In the tomb from Egypt, there are hundreds of boats with tiny people holding oars, to help the dead. I wonder who is helping them now that all their boats are here, all their tiny people. The caskets are empty. I'm sure this isn't what the Egyptians had in mind.

I hurry to find Dürer's prints, but it's really his face I was hoping to see, the painting with his long hair. The book that he touched is under glass. One room turns into another, and then the haystack is in front of me again. This time, its light enters my body like a beam between my breasts. When it makes me cry again, I'm worried a man in a dark suit like a guard is laughing at me. He's sitting in front of the painting, on a bench. I stand behind him to look in peace. It's raining outside, and I've got to get back to South Station, find the train line that goes to Newton, Boston College. I have to meet people I don't know—friends of my poetry publisher—and converse, sleep in their house. When I turn away, it's like turning away from the ocean.

So, I was rushing, but then the woman in the statue sees me. The Bodhisattva is made of carved gray limestone with traces of gilding—maybe that's what makes her shine—from the Northern

Zhou or early Sui dynasty. Her name is a nickname for Observing the Cries of the World. She's a mother. I don't know this when I see her in the oblong room, having hurried through one door to get through another, but her gaze is so loving it holds me at her feet. There is another disc below her waist, another in her dress, below her knees. I wonder how stone can be so full of kindness, of her. The house is on fire, but she's waiting on me, on everybody. She won't go until no one is suffering. I stay with her awhile. Veils fall from her wrists of her gown, like calm water. I don't touch her.

6.

On the train to Newton is a beautiful little girl in a purple coat. She's speaking a language I don't know, everyone's eyes averted. When I smile at her, her father, she whispers to him, points to another seat away from me. "No, no, we're okay here," he says in English. I try not to look at anyone, focus on fabric, canvas of a coat. It's already dark, near 5 p.m. I don't mean to cry, blink it away. Newton is bright even at night, gingerbread houses downtown. I find the house where I'm staying—a two-story, two-family house. Follow my directions to go around back, open the unlocked main door, go up the skinny wooden staircase banging my suitcase that barely fits between the walls, sticks in the corners. I can barely lug it up, my purse flying around my wrist. Sweating in the cold. It's just this one night here, and tomorrow night I fly out. I knock on the door of the people who are taking me in—two teachers, one a poet. They know almost nothing about me, except that their friend, Rick, director of the press that published my last two poetry collections, has asked them to help me.

The poet is very tall, her husband calm—both kind. Inviting me to sit with them, have dinner. He sits at the top of the table, and she's across from me. They ask if they can take my hands, say a prayer. When I give one hand to the husband, one to the wife, they hold onto me, making a circle. When the husband, uncertain, asks his wife if a particular prayer is okay, it's almost too much, their sweetness. But my heart has calmed down. After dinner, they come upstairs with me to my private apartment—office, bedroom, bath—and ask me to read to them, poems. And we trade readings—the poet and I, poem for poem. In some poems, she writes about Mary Magdalene. They sit on the other two couches, listening and asking me to read more. My bed is dozens of colors of pink and red in pillows and quilts, like the tiny flowers in fields.

There aren't many books on the city of Brockton. But I'd found someone who had written about towns all over America that had gone to ruin. And he'd written on Brockton. I'd been wanting to email him, to ask him how to find out if the city killed my son. But I couldn't decide how to phrase it—questions about illness and water, factories and shoes. I didn't want to bug him. It turned out that the author teaches at the same college as this couple. The poet knew him. Not well, but he was in her department. She said he didn't suffer fools. She asked if I had contacted him yet. When I said I hadn't, she said, "I'll just email him, and see if he can see you during his office hours." Which she did, before we went to sleep. For some reason, before she goes downstairs, I tell the poet about seeing Guanyin that afternoon. She says, "Another mother."

In the morning, the husband checked their email—"He wrote back," the husband said. The poet went over to the computer, and read the message. "He says that writing about Brockton is a fine thing for a poet to do." That sounded nice. "He's on sabbatical and not in the office, but he said for you to give him a call," the poet said. She wrote the number down. It took me all day to call. I'd walked to the college, seen the dead pile up in a Civil War exhibit. My son's pictures in my purse—the tapes, the locket. Right before

I left Newton, I sat on the couch upstairs, heart frantic again, called. He answered right away. "You're not the only one," he said, "to ask about this."

I'd told him my story briefly, explained my interest in the health of the city and potential links between its manufacturing history and illness, specifically childhood leukemia. When I'd mentioned that the ex-VP from Knapp Shoes had said that there had never been tanning of leather for shoes in Brockton, or even Massachusetts, he reminded me of one of the old shoe factory guys he'd written about in his essay on Brockton. How the guy said he could never get the yellow from the leather out of his hands. I wondered if he meant that that kind of stain could be a preface to others. But he didn't know where to tell me to look beyond the library, newspaper, local colleges—what I'm after isn't in his area of expertise. "You can't go to the boosters, the Chamber of Commerce, with this kind of thing," he said. His main advice, though, was to show up in person, look around. "Brockton," he said, "never disappoints."

7.

I'd thought it was a good thing to finally go to see my aunt and uncle, to say my son's name. A breakthrough, as my aunt had said. But not telling my family, the subterfuge, the not doing what other people wanted me to do—it cost me. Over the holidays, someone posted a link to a suicide prevention group—I clicked it and watched a video. A woman who had survived a suicide attempt explained that you can have something unresolved in your life, your past, something that lies low, but then something else can happen—a crisis—and it can uncover that sleeping thing too. She said it's important to remember that there are other ways to make the pain stop besides death.

In the weeks before I flew to see my aunt and uncle, some sleeping thing started to wake up. I felt darker and darker. I would overhear myself thinking, "You don't deserve to live." Or "You've had your life already. It's over now." I thought of death as sleeping, a nice sleep. This wasn't the suicidal ideation of my twenties, the long slow slide into a dark cavern. The thoughts were quick, brief, as if they'd slipped in from some outside source. I was worried. I knew it had something to do with taking action, with fear. It had to do with being Tommy's mother in the world, even though I still felt as though I wasn't allowed to be this, to say it out loud. To show up at his real parents' home and ask to know about his life.

So I decided that I would take actions, regardless of my feelings of fear. I'd already bought the plane ticket to Boston. I flew on Thanksgiving because it had the cheapest fare. I'd reserved an inexpensive hotel room for five nights, but when I did a budget and found I couldn't afford the hotel after all, I asked for help. I hate asking for help, for people to put me up. But I emailed my poetry publisher. I got the place in Newton for a night. I emailed Julia a few days before I was to leave, and she invited me to stay with them.

But by the time I was actually on the bus from Boston to my aunt and uncle's house, it wasn't just a set of isolated actions— drive car, check bag, buy bus ticket—I was about to enter a house full of people I barely knew, for no apparent reason. On the bus, I had that panic attack. Alone in the dark, I remembered my friend Janean had called me earlier on my cell. I called her back. I think she said she loved me. Maybe not, but I felt it anyway. Before I'd left home, I'd emailed my sponsor from the last town I'd lived in. I didn't have a new sponsor. Told her what I was going to do. She said that she was reminded that gratitude was an action. I knew she meant that I was expressing my gratitude toward my relatives, that I would thank them for raising my son. But I would be taking from them too—I knew my talking would hurt them. Still, I also thought of action, of the taking of action, as gratitude. Gratitude for being alive. I thought of action as good, like exercise, like lifting a weight.

I don't know how much I've hurt my relatives. The way my uncle seemed unanchored from whatever place he'd been in. Like someone drowning and still talking about Tommy for me, because I needed him too. I know he needed it too, but what if he couldn't take it? While I'd been staying at their house, we'd all learned that Anne was dying. The freezing of her body continuing. She'd been hospitalized. Julia sent me an email when I got back home, said she wouldn't have recognized Anne if my uncle hadn't gone in the room first. "She gave me a thumbs-up," Julia said. She said it was hard not to cry. They told Anne I'd been to visit, that I had a new book of poems. Anne typed on her machine. "She said she'd love to have any of your books," Julia said. "One of the nurses can read your poems to her." Anne had also typed, "Don't be sorry for me. I've had a good life." For Christmas, I sent a book to Julia to give to Anne, and a T-shirt with a dog saying for Julia, a mug with dog talk for Mark, and six dog biscuits wrapped in a bow. I didn't hear from them. I don't know if Anne is worse, or if they were expecting the tapes of Tommy made into a DVD (instead of my silly presents) or if my dad told them that I'm likely to write about them. Or what.

There is still another action to take—finding a place that can make the pre-videotape reels with Tommy into a DVD. It's something I can do for my aunt and uncle, something they couldn't do. That I can do because I love them. And it's what I was after from the beginning, to find my son. Who I now see in my face, and who is alive in the world of 1981 and 1982 on these tapes. I can go there pretty soon.

When I'd come home from the trip, gone back to work, I was

reluctant to talk about anything that happened, afraid I would talk it away. The way so many things can be talked away, minimized into anecdote by a listener, a commenter. But I thought of Kim, the poet, and her husband, whom I had stayed with in Newton. How talking to them, those kind strangers, how it hadn't been like that at all. When I'd returned home, I'd written them a note. Kim wrote back, said, "Frank brings up your visit as a sort of touchstone for change we want to make in our lives." She said, "I wouldn't have known that you were frazzled coming to my house. You were radiant."

Radiolarians

1.

In *Labyrinths*, Borges said "the night pleases us because it suppresses idle details, just as our memory does." The spiral mirroring the Milky Way, the underworld, even our bodies inside, our falling for many nights. That year in Massachusetts, before my son was born, I'd loved running at night, especially in snow. Starting at midnight when things quieted, past factories, empty highway, Dunkin' Donuts the only yellow light. That girl in the Bridgewater dorm warned me against running alone at night, but I'd always felt safe. Even with the prison nearby. At night the buildings in town became older, defined, each factory window empty and full with everyone who'd ever looked out year after year, each blink. The snow clearing a mirror.

But then in August 1979, I moved to Florida again, and couldn't run. Everything meant to burn, palmetto, pine needles, the sun kindling everyone into a drunken candle. I took sweltering walks at night past sand pits, the mall's cool air-conditioned hand, wearing Levi's, tube top, dollars in my pocket for a magazine. A man jogging ahead in jeans had seemed strange, chunky in a sweatshirt, too many clothes. But the sky was pink, there was a little breeze.

On my way home from the drugstore, I'd seen the jogger up ahead, he'd turned too, running the way we'd come. But then he'd disappeared. I was coming up on the 7-Eleven, remembered that they carried *Rolling Stone*, picked up the issue with Joni Mitchell on the cover, powdery, aging. Later, I guessed where the jogger had gone, understood the way he'd appeared like a figure in a board game, then vanished near the 7-Eleven. The back of the store secluded and dark. I thought of him there, overdressed, wondering why I didn't pass by his knife and the green Dumpster— imagining the ease of my wings folded, legs a basket, jumbled. Impatient, he'd run down the road ahead while I read in the store. He waited again, in the near dark close to my house. Ski mask, yellow hair like a broom sticking up, cut eyes, mouth.

When I turned the corner into my development, I saw him near a tall bush, almost a hedge, something to hide behind. When he spoke, I tasted how easily I could be leaves in a hidden place. Rain and blood, earth, where a body can go maneuvering between woods and bushes. His knife at my belly, diagramming an entrance, while I kept near the white center line. I was losing ground until a car came, scared him off, headlights bright as snow.

If time is the soul of the world, then this moment must be somewhere. My moments of escape. Is all time somewhere? The tapes I have of Tommy (Tom? I no longer know what name to call him), is the time on them somewhere too, playing over and over? Is he alive somewhere? I've had the tapes for more than a month. I asked a couple of people at work if they knew where I could get them converted to DVD. Just asking Nick and then Nancy about it, getting the question out, was slow going. I felt as if I was deep underwater, exhausted by each word. "Call Speedway," Nancy said, "They'll know." When the weather turns cold, I put the tapes in my childhood dresser, protect them with my clothes.

I tell myself the tapes could be brittle, they could be ruined if handled. I think that as long as I have the tapes, he's alive on them, even if I can't see him.

Five hundred million years ago, radiolarians lived in the ocean. The fossils of their single cells tell how old rocks are in the deep ocean. Fossil, from the Welsh *bedd,* meaning grave. The beds of the radiolarians. Their skeletons of silica in the beach sand. How far back does time start? Every time I go back to Orlando, I feel as though I'm walking through my past. One of the last times there, I just wanted to sit in my old driveway and the house was gone, just gone, a swath of grass. As if they'd taken who I'd been in that house—me and the Sugar Mountain man along with the boards and nails. I'd been with Nick from the artists' residency center. We were in a van, bringing three of the artists to Orlando for a salon in a patron's home. As we drove by the empty lot, I'd turned to Nick in the driver's seat, said I used to live there. Dismayed. Nick had said, "Let it go," very matter of factly, as someone who is fifty and has let a lot of things go can say it. But I still see our bodies, our hair, our hands on each other in the mouth of an earthmover, crumpling easily like dolls into one of those big trucks full of dirt, off to the burial, the bed. I wondered how it could be left behind like sawdust, peanut shells on the floor, like those songs sung in a room, and then just left there when he walked out the door.

The magnetic field of the earth is comforting, the way it keeps the sun from burning us up. Solar winds passing by. Without it, we could have been another Mars, everything on fire. It's a miracle anything's here. One night I sleep almost twelve hours, wake up, call Speedway. "You want Carlton in South Daytona," a man said, "but thanks for calling us first. Here's the number." I call, leave a message. A girl calls me back. I describe my reels. "Are they all about an inch and a half?" she asks. "It sounds like you have two hundred fifty feet of film." She says, "We can do it. We say a week, but usually it's two days." "Thanks," I say. "Thanks." Dave Carlton can convert the tapes into something I can see. "He gets here at seven in the morning, even though we open at nine. You can knock on the door."

2.

In 2009, *Boston Magazine* doesn't seem to do its surveys rating quality of life anymore. Instead, the cities are in competition for specific categories, like "Do-It-Yourselfer." Brockton wins in the category of "The Sports Fan." I can't find the earlier article I'd seen from the late 1990s, the high rates of childhood leukemia I thought I'd found. Instead, using Brockton's Mortality Records from 2005–2007, I find that the Massachusetts Department of Public Health reported fifteen leukemia deaths in the city. One of these deaths was a child. I'm surprised. Was I wrong about the numbers? About the city? My intuition—was that off too? It's good news for everyone, but I'm still stunned.

Using the 2004–2006 Calendar Year Hospital Discharges record, the Massachusetts Community Health Information Profile counted twenty-five leukemia hospitalizations in Brockton. Leukemia incidence was drawn from the 2001–2005 Cancer Registry. MassCHIP reported a total leukemia incidence of forty-seven. None of these are children. I don't know if I am reading the profile correctly, so I send an email to MassCHIP, ask for the most recent Leukemia Report for Brockton. The director sends me directions to download the software and an imbedded tutorial to form queries and retrieve historical date on cancer incidence in Brockton from 1985 to 2005, hospitalization data from 1989 to 2006, and mortality data from 1989 to 2007. He says it will be worth my time to download if I will need the data on a regular basis. The data includes births, deaths, cancer incidence, hospitalizations, ER data, substance abuse treatment, admissions, HIV/AIDS incidence and prevalence, STDs, et cetera. I wonder who he thinks I am that I would need access to this data on a regular basis.

Then, he says, "A technical note: there are too few cases of childhood leukemia in Brockton in an individual year for us to release the number without threatening to violate confidentiality. You can get past this by forming groups of years (e.g., 1985–1987) using the group function in MassCHIP." He tells me to disable my firewall to form groups of years. He's very helpful, even kindly. There are too few cases? In every year? I don't know. What made me think it was high? Did I misread that quality of life survey? See a number on one line that belonged on another?

I start to look at the health of the city, the water. According to Sperling's Best Places, Brockton rates a 27 in Water Quality (100 is best; U.S. average is 55). In Air Quality, Brockton got 28 out of 100 (U.S. is 48). For Superfund Sites, Brockton got a 30 out of 100 (U.S. is 71). The Superfund number is based upon the number and impact of EPA Superfund pollution sites in the county, including spending on the cleanup. When I looked up the Environmental Justice Report for Plymouth County, I found that the most common contaminant detected at this Superfund site was ethylbenzene. I remembered benzene from another report, "Childhood Cancer in New Jersey: 1979–1995." It noted that "some parental occupational exposures have been suggested as risk factors for childhood leukemia. Maternal exposures include benzene."

The Superfund site in Plymouth County is next door to Brockton, on three acres in Bridgewater, where I went to school the year before I got pregnant. The Cannon Engineering Corporation (CEC) is the Superfund site. It was cleaned up in December 1982, a year before the date my son got an earache, when he started to get sick. But I don't see a direct connection from this to my son's illness. I saw that the EPA found that "from 1974 to 1980, CEC was licensed to transport, store, and incinerate certain types of hazardous wastes. [As of December 1982] on-site structures include 21 storage tanks, three buildings, an office/warehouse, and an incinerator. Ground water south of the site is contaminated with benzene, 1.1.1-trichloroethane, and toluene. To date, no contamination of drinking wells has been detected. A pond to the south and a swamp to the west are also contaminated. Owners of CED were indicted for illegal storage and disposal of hazardous wastes. In October 1982, the state contracted for removal and disposal of hazardous wastes in tanks (about 150,000 gallons) and in about 600 drums." The on-site air, the groundwater, and the soil and sediments contained VOCS—a suspected carcinogen. The site is thirty minutes from where I went to school, forty-four minutes from where my son lived. But it's cleaned up, fenced off. And according to the EPA, Plymouth County has a "good" Superfund rating as of 2004, with just the one site.

A 2008 study says that Brockton ranks in the "top 10 most extensively environmentally overburdened communities in Massachusetts (out of 362 communities)." Brockton "grossly exceeds" the statewide average of 166 environmental hazard points per community, with 709 points. There are 347 hazardous waste sites in the city—"an average of over 16 hazardous waste sites per square mile." The study says that "exposure to industrial chemicals is also believed by scientists to be contributing to dramatic increases since the 1950s in cancers—an epidemic that kills half-a-million Americans each year." The author says that cancer "now kills more American children that any other single disease for the first time in history." But a public health official at Northeastern University tells me that nationally, cancer doesn't meet the public health definition of an "epidemic." She also gives me the rates for childhood leukemia incidence in Brockton, and they are very similar to the rates for Massachusetts as a whole. She mentions that this doesn't take into account geographic clusters of leukemia incidence in Brockton, but she says clusters are very difficult to determine.

I don't know if this old mill city made my son sick. How can I know? It seems ridiculous, my collecting bits of information on leukemia and potential toxins. Still, the town is poor, people get sick. It's obvious the water quality is pretty low. But low quality and carcinogenic aren't the same thing. The violent crime rate is 7 out of 10, with 10 being the worst. How many things can a town worry about at once? And what am I after? If children aren't sick, why am I looking here? I'd thought that environmental hazards in this city could have caused Tommy's leukemia. I still feel that the city made him sick, but it's intuitive—I can't prove it. I'd wanted to know why he died. I'd also wanted to know if I'm responsible. When I thought that after Tommy's death other children were dying from leukemia in Brockton, it seemed a crime to be passive. Were more lives at stake? How could I be quiet? A mother would find out what killed her son. But the data doesn't show a citywide rate much different from the rest of the state. The public health official had mentioned that there could be pockets, cancer clusters, but that they're hard to identify. The city is starting to feel like a dead end. What I've always wanted is to find him.

In a photograph of children in the tenement district of Brockton in December 1940, I recognize the scene. It has the blue clarity of winter. Not a cloud in the sky. It's where my dad lived, my grandmother, even my uncle for a while—the ghetto of Brockton.

The tenement house has long, sash windows, bracketed cornices. The roof curves like a slate slide. In front of the identical house next door (except for the one black shade instead of green, a radio in the window, and no children or dog) is a blue 1930 Model A Ford Tudor Sedan, stripped, with a blackened passenger-side door as if the car had been set on fire. There are eight small children, an adolescent boy, and maybe one grown man, plus the dog who paws the street. Bare branches spring from the ground instead of trees. No women are here. It doesn't look as though there is anywhere to go. Just the gray porch steps, the gray street, or back inside the house, which looks abandoned, night-black. My dad grew up here. Except for the time in Wellfleet, he was mostly in this place when he was young. I don't know why this past looks so familiar. Maybe I should get out of Brockton, let this place go.

3.

The video place is in a short strip mall; a girl sits at a desk in the corner of the room. "Did you call?" she asks. I have the tapes in a plastic bag. She takes them out, reads the black Magic Marker on the white cartridges. She stacks the numbered "First Birthday" tapes in a tower, chronologically. "These are Super 8's," she said. There's a lot of crowded writing on the last tape—mention of another child—so I read the beginning to her: "It's Plymouth Beach, five months." She places it on top of the stack.

"I was worried the tape might be brittle," I said. She removes the cover, exposes the thin film, holds it to her nose.

"I'm smelling it because when Super 8 goes bad, there's a chemical reaction. There's a tape over there that's ruined." She nods toward another desk in the other corner—someone else's tape. "Yours are good," she said. Fifty feet on each reel is between two and a half and three and a half minutes of film. I have five tapes. I might have fifteen minutes of my son's life. I don't want to tell her that, but I want her to be careful.

"It's precious to us," I say. "It's someone who died." She wants to know what to write on the label she'll put on the DVD.

"We usually just put 'Family Memories.'" I give her the name on his birth certificate, his grave: "Thomas Edward Smith."

"The Early Years?" she asks. Suggesting I add this. Did I not tell her this was someone who died? Maybe she thinks he died older, that he had an adult life.

"Just his name," I say. I'm thinking of Mark and Julia, of them opening my envelope with the DVD and reading the label. "Is there any way I could get the DVD by the end of the day on Friday?" Otherwise it'll be Monday, and I'll be back to work. I'd have to get it before work, keep it in my purse all day, wait until I got home to see him.

"Yes, I think so. I just finished a job. I should be able to do it."

I was thinking there would be sound on the tapes, but at home, when I call my friend, she says, "No, there's no sound." I was hoping I might hear his voice. I look up Super 8 mm film. It turns out there was an environmentally hazardous Super 8 with sound, developed in 1973. A magnetic strip recorded it. I don't know if mine had sound. I'd asked my friend if I'd be able to see my son's face on the DVD.

"Do you remember the film strips in school?" she asked.

"That kind of blinking film?"

"Yes," she said.

4.

Each of the Super 8's had writing on them: Plymouth Beach 5 months/ Tommy Smith & Mikie 8 months; Tommy 1st Birthday (1 of 4); Tommy 1st Birthday (2 of 4); Tommy 1st Birthday (3 of 4); Tommy 1st Birthday (4 of 4). On the way home from dropping off the tapes, I turn on the radio. There's a tornado watch. "The storm is right over US 1 near Ponce Inlet." I'm on US 1, driving into it, according to the radio. Then I can see it, darkness to my left, over the bridge. Covering the condo towers beside the north bridge. "In five minutes it could be out to sea," the radio voice had said. I keep driving into it. I wonder what it would be like—if the dark sky picks me up in its hands. The next day a woman in Cocoa Beach, where the tornado did touch down, will say that it squeezed her house in and out, like an accordion.

Waiting for the video girl to call me the next day, to say I can pick up the tapes, I drive to the post office. I brake at the end of my street, at the roundabout. A car passes. I go. I never see the giant black SUV until its horn is blaring. Look out my driver's side window to see it has just stopped from hitting me. It's disorienting. I'm a little worried about the drive to South Daytona. The video girl left a message in the few minutes I was out. The tapes are ready. I make myself eat something, a yogurt. I go get the DVD.

The cover says "Treasured Memories" in fancy script. The DVD is labeled "Thomas Edward Smith" and underneath "Home Movies." When the disc loads, the background is designed to look like those old film screens with the numbers counting down before the movie begins. It has a big 5 in a circle with radiating lines that come from inside the curve of the number, a kind of sun. But the numbers don't count down—it's decorative. Above it, in thick black letters, it reads: "A Night At The Movies." Who thought of that? There is no night. My son's name appears again in a starred box, slightly off kilter with the letters lifting up to the right. And underneath, "Play Movie." Along the right edge, and lightly scattered on the left edge, in the corners, is a charring, like sand. As if the tape were burning up. Ruin a part of the design.

My son appears, leaning back against Julia in her black bathing suit. He is standing on the sand, the water just visible in the background. He's wearing white shorts, a short-sleeved blue shirt. He's watching another boy—the Mikie whose name was markered on the tape, I imagine, though I don't know who he is, or who the bearded man is who holds him. Mikie seems more retiring than Tommy, who looks ready to launch himself at Mikie, to play. And though Mikie is three months older than Tommy, he's smaller, more tentative. There is a horrifying soundtrack playing. No one asked if I wanted music. The video girl CHOSE music for the DVD. It's bombastic, big band. Julia holds onto Tommy while he walks around, faces the camera, smiles. He is such a big boy. Julia rubs his back while he looks at the sand. Another child, a boy of about five with straight black hair, blocks the camera, dancing in place.

The camera spans the beach. It's August 1981. The bearded man holds his nervous baby. A big blue tarp on poles makes a tent for Julia, for the playpen. Next to it is a black truck. A slower kind of dance music plays, something from the '30s or '40s, and there's a close-up of Tommy and Mikie in the playpen. Tommy is in motion, reaching for Mikie and a little off balance, hands behind him steadying him as he reaches. He's five months old. He looks as if he's kissing the top of Mikie's head, holding it like a pumpkin. Tommy pulls at the collar of Mikie's shirt. Mikie looks distressed. Someone holds a doll out to Mikie, and then to Tommy, who smiles a big smile, eyes bright. Looking up. I get so confused when he looks up—it's like looking at myself, in him. He is sweetly chubby—his face, his arms, legs.

Julia takes him into the water. His head is resting on her shoulder, facing the shore. He's wearing a white baseball cap. One of his arms, a hand, rests against the skin of her back. In a blurry space, I can see her fingers around his legs, keeping him safe, close to her body. She's looking out to sea. She's laughing. Mark is holding Mikie while the bearded man holds the hand of the older child. The water is above their knees, to their thighs. It's a beautiful day, blue sky, sun. And then it's over.

The Floating Island

The light is yellow, inside the hospital. Someday this will be an ancient kingdom. Someday this will be a sea. Julia is smiling, seated facing the camera. Mark appears from a space beyond, a nurse's station or a hallway. Beside Julia, a massive cord hangs, as if there is a giant phone on the wall beside her. My son is on her lap.

A man says that time is not a river, we don't stop at different places. The future isn't down below. It's a construct, he says. We're making it up. There's water behind him, a river that doesn't fall. My son is in the Floating Hospital. He's in the Floating Children's Cancer Center. As if the children themselves float—as if cancer makes them float.

First there was a boat in Boston Harbor in 1894 with women and sick children riding around on it. A hospital on the water because a minister thought the ocean air would help children heal. It floated for thirty-three years. When it burned, they built a building on land, called it the same name. It has a state-of-the-art bone marrow transplant unit which I might have personally experienced. My marrow, the deepest part, stars in the field of his body. If there had been some increase in his health, if he'd been strong enough. "You were going to get a call," Julia had said. "You were going to be the donor."

We're back where we started, in a hospital.

All the chubbiness has gone out of his face, his body. His eyes look ten times larger. If you put the picture of him at five months beside this one of him at one year, sick in the hospital, on March 17, 1982, two months and ten days before he dies, I don't think you would have any idea that this is the same child. How is it that he still looks like me? How did I stay? As if I'd never left him. Look in his eyes. There I am.

The big band music plays briefly. Tommy puts a red lollipop in his mouth. Julia shakes his other hand hello. As Nana Smith bends down to see his face, and he looks up at her, "Somewhere Over the Rainbow" plays without words. This is what I have instead of his voice. It almost looks like they can hear it too. He smiles so much, so contentedly. He's still such a peaceful baby, like when he was born.

I hoped that by writing about Tommy, I could find him. That the writing would take me to him. But still, I'm surprised that that is what it's doing.

I'd decided to write about his birth from memory, to begin with what had been unforgettable. But when I finally read my diary from that day, I saw that I had held him twice, not once. He'd been born at 2:13 a.m., and the nurse woke me to hold him at 9 a.m. and to feed him at 1 p.m. Twice. In my memory it is all one holding. *I talked to you very quietly, but I don't know what I said. I think it was just my talking that was important—you knew me already.* Even then, right after, I didn't know what words I said.

When the nurse woke me up, told me to follow her, I'd fallen instead. Fainted. I can remember it now, the smell of ammonia— smelling salts, the cold floor on my body through the cotton gown. Trying to follow the nurse and slipping away into the dark. Getting up. Swaying while I waited for my baby. *I unwrapped your white blanket, touched your fingers and toes.*

For two days, I have to use ice packs on my breasts—they are so full. Once a doctor told me that I was made for having babies, the space between my hips a perfect house. I was made for this. The body is the hull of a ship, the place where music comes from, sun and moon, the stars are bodies, the garment that covers.

I didn't know I could change my mind. I didn't know I could keep you.

I've sent an email to Mark and Julia to see if my box arrived at Christmas. I'd checked the tracking, and my address had been undeliverable. Someone picked it up at the post office. Julia writes me right back, forwards me her original response. I see my name is spelled wrong in the email address she used. I imagine that Kelly with a "y" is happier than me, living in a house of her own. Julia said she loved the "Love a Dog" T-shirt that I sent her, that every day Mark uses the coffee mug with dog talk that I'd sent (every day), that the dogs ate the treats in two seconds.

A card comes in the mail from a friend in New York. The image on the cover is a letter of van Gogh's written around his drawing in the center of the page. A sketch of "Wheat Field with Setting Sun." I don't know why I'm surprised his letter is in French, that I can only understand a few words. Somehow I'd assumed we spoke the same language. There is a place in the center of my chest where his picture reaches—it's so direct. The words around it like a song I don't know.

Julia is tying a low necklace on Tommy—sort of a lei, yellow flowers. He doesn't mind, he hardly seems to feel it. She kisses him on his neck, looks at his face to see if it has made him smile, kisses him again. Looks, kisses him again. How have his eyes become so big? Wide open all the time. He has sort of a cast on one of his arms. Maybe something is being injected. His arm is stabilized with a kind of board underneath, thick white strips over it, gauze. He doesn't seem to mind it.

I spend most of the day at the window where you are, under the nurses' stares. Behind the glass, all the newborns lie side by side in plastic cribs. Two babies were born the same morning as you, three others born the day after. When I feel too weak to stand anymore, I walk back to the bed. Get stronger, go back to the glass. Sometimes the nurses pull the blinds on me. It is an awful feeling, knowing you are right behind those blinds, and I can't see you.

The camera spans the hospital room walls which are covered in cards. The film is kind of fuzzy here, but I see a duck. I don't know who they are from. I didn't send a card. Didn't know that I could or even where the hospital was until this year. I don't know how many cards—fifty? Seventy-five? It's one whole wall. "Happy Birthday Tommy" is written on three cards, one word each, and hung in an arc from the ceiling. Horrifyingly, a disco version of "Somewhere Over the Rainbow" begins to play, but calms down, becomes just a speedy version of the song. Julia holds Tommy up in his yellow hospital outfit, and he smiles. I see two teeth on top, two on the bottom.

The nurses told Dr. Treharne I'd been abusing my privilege of looking through the glass. When he examined me, he was silent. He left, forgetting to open the gray privacy curtain circling my bed.

There's a flower that looks like a corsage, very green, that Julia takes out of a plastic container. Something for a prom, a marriage. She brushes it against the side of his face. But he really just wants the green lollipop the bearded man beside him is unwrapping. I think he may be Julia's brother? Julia is in a rocking chair. I can feel his smile when he gets the lollipop.

Mark wheels Tommy in a highchair, up to a table set in the hallway of the hospital. He is crying at the commotion, but Mark is laughing slightly, as if it is so unusual for Tommy to cry, to protest. And then he's at the head of the table happily eating. The table almost blocks the entire hallway. Sometimes a nurse walks past. Then I see a woman I don't know smiling at Tommy, she bends down and talks to him a long time, laughing, smiling. It's Ellen. It's the old woman I met in Falmouth, Mark's aunt Ellen. She's beaming down there with her knees bent, her hand on her chin, looking from Tommy to Mark and smiling.

Nana Smith looks right into the camera with an expression of fright. She's sitting beside Mark. Julia on the other side. Both flanking Tommy, who is smiling very big. First Julia pretends to take something from his closed mouth, touching his lips; then, Mark does this. And both times, he looks at each of them with such tenderness, such love. They all move so slowly, as if they are underwater. Julia's arm reaching toward him, the tiny red flower of his mouth. His head bowed slightly in a shy joy of knowing the game they are playing, eyes looking up at her smiling. When Mark reaches for him, Tommy gives him the same bowed head, the same calm tenderness.

It's this moment that makes me think I should protect them, not send them the DVD. But protecting other people is where all the trouble started—the arrogance of deciding what another person needs. And what could I save them from? His love? Asleep in a drawer for almost thirty years. It was the only thing they'd asked of me. "We couldn't do it." Turn the Super 8's into something they can see. They want to see him alive in the world.

Later, Julia is rocking Tommy on her shoulder. His face is watching the camera, eyes open. There is a small distress on his face, but as she rocks him, his whole expression changes. His eyes relax, his smile comes back. And she is smiling with her mouth closed—there is a contentedness in her face as she rocks him, even in this terrible time, even as he's dying, she gives him all her happiness. She looks like a woman who knows what she's doing, the corsage now on her blouse. The film shifts to Mark rocking Tommy against his chest. Tommy asleep, head tilted upward on Mark's white shirt, mouth open. That contentment is in Mark's face too, contained joy, a small smile, but I can feel it—how happy he is to have Tommy asleep in his arms.

In another frame, I'm not sure what I'm seeing. Tommy doesn't have the yellow outfit on anymore. There seems to a square board affixed to his lower leg. Nana Smith holds her fist to her mouth. Julia covers the board with a blanket. Everyone's shoulders are bent, everyone is bending forward toward the floor. *I can feel your foot kicking—I can see it moving under my skin.*

Then Tommy is in Mark's arms. He'll die in his arms.

The camera pans the presents, the cakes—there are two. One reads "Happy Birthday Tommy" and has a merry-go-round in the corner. There are flowers inside a bear vase, and the camera focuses on an unreadable card. A green creature on the wall has a yellow balloon in his hand that reads "Happy Birthday Tom." Tommy has a Mickey Mouse birthday hat on his head. He's wearing a new outfit—it looks like a white- and blue-striped baseball player's uniform, but there's a colorful animal on the pocket. Julia takes his hands, and he walks over to the big cake, touches the merry-go-round, the frosting. And then he turns around, walks into Julia's arms. Mikie is there is a dark suit. Standing by himself. He looks bigger than Tommy now, taller. Nurses are crowded into the little room outside, across the hallway. The station. They don't wear nurses' outfits. Maybe one of them is his doctor—she was a woman, Beth Gleghorn. She was doing her residency—young then. The women are watching the sick baby. They want to make him smile.

Tommy pushes his hat away. I can see Julia say, "Oh," and laugh when it comes off. He sits with his ankles crossed on Julia's lap and eats little bites of cake from his paper plate. Time has passed—Julia now has a sweater on over her long-sleeved blouse. There are flowers in the upper-right corner. Mikie leans against an armchair, looking nervous like Nana. They both eat their cake off the same tiny table, not speaking to each other.

A clown in a yellow hat, tie, and pants is twisting balloons in front of Tommy. I can see the clown is a bit much for him, but he's polite, leaning back into Julia, watching the show. The clown has red dots on his tie, his shirt, a red nose. He looks diseased. Mikie, on the other side of the room, has both fists covering his shut eyes.

But Mark and Julia are smiling, the clown is drawing a face on a tiny white balloon, and Tommy is smiling at someone across the room (good-bye, good-bye). Maybe Ellen, the beaming Ellen. Nana Smith is smiling now too, smoothing her blouse down. The clown has made a balloon bee with black wings that Julia buzzes around Tommy's head, but he barely notices, smiling at the person across the room. He turns. For a moment, he sees me.

Notes

epigraphs

From Brenda Hillman's "Small Spaces" in *Bright Existence* (Middletown, CT: Wesleyan University Press, 1993). Reprinted by permission.

Zonas, "Charon," in *Dances for Flute and Thunder: Poems from the Ancient Greek*, trans. Brooks Haxton (New York: Viking, 1999). Reprinted by permission.

Constellation

Anonymous, *Go Ask Alice* (Englewood Cliffs, NJ: Prentice-Hall, 1971).

Seven Works of Mercy

Caravaggio, *The Seven Works of Mercy*, 1607 (oil on canvas, 390 X 260 cm, Church of Pio Monte della Misericordia, Naples).

The Last Time I Saw Her

The epigraph is from Samuel Beckett's poem "Cascando," written in 1936. *Collected Poems in English and French* (New York: Grove Press, 1977).

The story from *The Paris Review* is Rudy Wilson's "Impressions" (Spring 1984).

Regency

Source for the information on Edward Keaton's crime and sentence: Debbie Salamone, "Career Criminal Gets Life for Kidnapping, Forced Sex." *Orlando Sentinel*, 10 Nov. 1995.

The quote, "Covered with the shadow of it," is from Psalm 80:10, *King James Bible*.

Notes

Broadway

Source for the quotes: Charlotte Davis Kasl, *Women, Sex, and Addiction: A Search for Love and Power* (New York: Ticknor & Fields, 1989), p. 205.

Palindrome

The two quotes are from *Volume Two: An Angel at My Table* (originally published in 1984) in Janet Frame's *An Autobiography* (New York: George Braziller, 1991), pp. 233 and 248.

How to Make a Shoe

A 2006 online exhibition, "The Brockton Shoe Industry," Stonehill College Archives and Special Collections, was consulted for information on shoemaking.

Source for the *Boston Phoenix* quote: Camille Dodero, "Decay Artist." *Boston Phoenix*, 28 June 2006.

1982

Source for the quotes: Lynn S. Baker, *You and Leukemia: A Day at a Time* (Philadelphia: W. B. Saunders Company, 1978).

Informant

The quote is from an original, unpublished poem written by Kelle Groom written in 1989 and inspired by "The Girl Without Hands" from *The Complete Grimm's Fairy Tales* (New York: Random House, 1972).

Guanyin

The essay referred to is "Rocky Marciano's Ghost," from *Good with Their Hands: Boxers, Bluesmen, and Other Characters from the Rust Belt* by Carlo Rotella (Berkeley: University of California Press, 2002).

Radiolarians

In section 2, the following sources were consulted:

Massachusetts Department of Public Health, Massachusetts Community Health Information Profile: "Leukemia Report for Brockton"; "City/Town Cancer Profile (2002–2006) for Brockton"; "Kids Count Profile"; "Health Status Indicators Report for Brockton."

Notes

Daniel R. Faber and Eric J. Krieg, "Unequal Exposure to Ecological Hazards: Environmental Injustices in the Commonwealth of Massachusetts," *Environmental Health Perspectives*, Vol. 110, Supp. 2, April 2002, pp. 277–88.

CDC, MMWR Weekly, "Trends in Childhood Cancer Mortality—United States, 1990–2004," Dec. 7, 2007.

Charles Duhigg, "Clean Water Laws Are Neglected, at a Cost in Suffering," *New York Times*, 13 Sept. 2009.

Charles Duhigg, "That Tap Water Is Legal but May Be Unhealthy," *New York Times*, 17 Dec. 2009. Link to "Toxic Water: A series about the worsening pollution in American waters and regulators response" provides national database of water pollution violations. Interactive version showed current violations in Brockton (two contaminants above legal limits; six contaminants found within legal limits) and Bridgewater, MA (one contaminant—tetrachloroethylene, a pollutant from dry cleaning and various industrial factories; nine contaminants within legal limits): www.nytimes.com/toxicwaters

In section 2, the quote from the report on childhood cancer in New Jersey is from the following source: Rachel Weinstein, et al., "Childhood Cancer in New Jersey 1979–1995," chapter II: Rates and Risk Factors for Specific Childhood Cancers, http://www.state.nj.us/health/cancer/child/index.html.

In section 2, the information from *Sperling's Best Places* is from the following source: http://www.bestplaces.net/City/Brockton-Massachusetts.aspx.

In section 2, the information on the Superfund site in Plymouth County is from the following source: U.S. Environmental Protection Agency, "Waste Site Cleanup & Reuse in New England," Plymouth, Massachusetts, http://www.epa.gov/region1/cleanup/resource/index.html.

In section 2, the quotes from the study are from the following report: Daniel R. Faber, "The Proposed Brockton Power Plant: Environmental Disparities in Brockton, MA," 27 March 2008.

The public health official referred to is Neenah Estrella-Luna, MPH, PhD, Northeastern University, Massachusetts. A public health professional and social justice activist, she provided extensive and patient assistance, including retrieval of historical data on cancer incidence in Brockton, interpretation of the data, and lengthy correspondence with me on cancer incidence in children nationally, as well as specifically in Brockton.

Acknowledgments

All my gratitude and love to those who believed in and supported this book. Special thanks to Bill Clegg for his brilliance and passion and beautiful way of seeing. Thank you to Dominick Anfuso, Amber Qureshi, Alessandra Bastagli, and Nicole Kalian at Free Press for bringing my work into the world with such expert care, and to Teresa Leo, Terry Ann Thaxton, and Linda Frysh—dear friends and fellow writers who generously read drafts and innumerable revisions over the last four years. Thank you to Michael Burkard for his early encouragement of this work, and to Mike M., Mary P., Ray, Janet, Richard McCann and the writers in his FAWC workshop, Rick Campbell, Simen Johan, Kim and Frank Garcia, Don Stap, Lynn and Jerry Schiffhorst, Amber Flora Thomas, Laurel McNear, Ann Brady, Beth Greenfield, Alan Felsenthal, Guy Lebeda, Judy Bolton-Fasman, Kelly Cherry, and Terri Witek.

My thanks to the editors who published selections from this memoir before it was completed, sending light my way: Sven Birkerts and William Pierce at *AGNI* for accepting the first chapter I'd written and nominating it for a Pushcart Prize, Margot Livesey and guest editor Kathryn Harrison at *Ploughshares*, Amber Withycombe at *Witness,* Paula Closson Buck at *West Branch*, Reamy Jansen at *Bloomsbury Review,* Dinty Moore at *Brevity,* Ann Neelon at *New Madrid,* and Todd Zuniga at *Opium.*

Grants and fellowships from the State of Florida, Division of

Cultural Affairs; the Atlantic Center for the Arts; and the Virginia Center for the Creative Arts supported the research and writing of this book. For research assistance, my thanks to Neenah Estrella-Luna, MPH, PhD at Northeastern University and to Nicole Tourangeau, Archivist and Special Collections Librarian at Stonehill College.

Finally, much love to my family: to my parents and my brother for their joy that this book exists, despite the darkness it reveals. My deep gratitude to my aunt and uncle for being my son's parents, for loving him so much, and for trusting me to tell his story.

About the Author

Kelle Groom is the author of three poetry collections and has been published in *The New Yorker* and *Ploughshares,* among other magazines. Her work was included in *Best American Poetry 2010* and has received special mention in the *Pushcart Prize* and *Best American Non-Required Reading* anthologies. She lives in Florida.